W9-BAV-474

THE JOHN HARVARD LIBRARY

Howard Mumford Jones

Editor-in-Chief

THE

Continental Harmony

By

WILLIAM BILLINGS

Edited by Hans Nathan

THE BELKNAP PRESS OF HARVARD UNIVERSITY PRESS · CAMBRIDGE, MASSACHUSETTS

1 9 6 1

Distributed in Great Britain by Oxford University Press, London

Library of Congress Catalog Card Number 61–13734

Printed in the United States of America

CONTENTS

CONTENTS

INTRODUCTION

In a readable and informative book, *America's Music: from the Pilgrims to the Present* (1955), Gilbert Chase distinguishes three phases of musical development in this country — preparation, expansion, fulfillment. Discussing the period of preparation, which for him runs to 1800, he distinguishes among gentlemen amateurs like Franklin and Francis Hopkinson, professional emigrants who came here to earn a livelihood, and native pioneers who, avoiding the dilettante approach, were in a real sense the first American composers. Among them are James Lyon, Andrew Law, Daniel Read, Timothy Swan, Samuel Holyoke, Oliver Holden, Supply Belcher (known as "the Handel of Maine"), Jeremiah Ingalls, and William Billings; and it is remarkable that practically all of them were New England men, a fact that throws an interesting sidelight on the supposed narrowness of the "Puritan" tradition. One name among these worthies that has vitality today is that of William Billings (1746–1800), whose tunes were sung in American churches late in the nineteenth century, whose "Chester" was played in the Revolutionary army, whose "Berlin" forms the basis of Ross Lee Finney's "Variations, Fugueing and Rondo" (1943), and another of whose hymn tunes is basic to Otto Luening's "Prelude on a Hymn Tune by William Billings." Part of Billings' importance to us is that his music has seemed to contemporary American composers so indigenous and in some ways so close to their own idiom that they have incorporated it into their own works.

We know too little about the first important American composer to do more than guess the kind of man he was. He was born in Boston, he had a scanty education, and he was a tanner by trade when he began composing music. He seems also to have been physically unattractive. One arm was withered, one leg was shorter than the other, he was blind in one eye, his voice was loud and harsh, and (possibly because of the tannery) he was said to be slovenly in dress and in appearance. Nevertheless he won the attention of Samuel Adams and other Boston ministers, and he became a recognized singing teacher, much in demand by local churches like the fashionable Brattle Street Church (where he taught briefly), one whose music was often performed and anthologized. In 1770 he published *The New-England Psalm-Singer*, engraved by no less a person than Paul Revere; and this he revised and, he thought, improved as *The Singing-Master's Assistant* (1778), a work that went through as many as three editions. After three other books (*Music in Miniature*, 1779; *The Psalm-Singer's Amusement*, 1781; and *The Suffolk Harmony*, 1786) he published in 1794 one of the most charming of early American music books, *The Continental Harmony*, here reproduced. Although he died poor, it cannot be said that he was a neglected genius for his vogue and influence in New England were wide. Dr. William Bentley of Salem, one of the few sound linguists in America, wrote in his diary that Billings "may justly be considered as the father of our New England music. Many who have imitated have excelled him, but none of them had better original powers."[1]

In December 1790, *The Massachusetts Magazine* in an article on "musick" remarked that:

> The present, indeed, seems to be an era for improvement in musick as well as in other arts; and makers of *tunes* as well of *poems*, and other mental as well as manual manufactures, have been numerous in some of the American states.

This seems to point to an unusual activity in the musical world of Massachusetts at that time, an assumption confirmed by the interest of Isaiah Thomas of Worcester, well known for his publishing ventures in a number of fields, in bringing out music books for churches and for other groups. Thus Thomas published in 1786 *The Worcester Collection of Sacred Music*, the "advertisement" of which tells us not only that Billings was "the first person we know of that attempted to compose Church Musick, in the New-England states," but also that "several adepts in musick" have followed his example. Not surprisingly, then, we find that Isaiah Thomas and Ebenezer T. Andrews published Billings' *The Continental Harmony*. American music was of course derivative, but in reference to psalm-tunes the Puritan tradition was rather more independent than is commonly supposed, and music of this sort was popular enough to justify the printing of more than a hundred "tune-books" (that is, if we do not include re-issues and single pieces) between the 1760's and the earlier years of the nineteenth

[1] *The Diary of William Bentley, D.D.* (Salem, Mass., 1907), vol. 2, entry of Sept. 28, 1800.

century. *The Continental Harmony* belongs, then, to a considerable library.

Like any other publication of its kind, it is divided into two parts: an exposition of musical theory, and the music itself, which consists of psalm-tunes (some of them "fuges"), a few pieces (possibly covered by the term "chorusses") in the same stylistic category but based on other than versified psalm-texts, as well as several anthems. That all of these compositions were "NEVER BEFORE PUBLISHED," as the frontispiece claims, must be qualified. "Connection,"[2] printed at the opening of the book in the form of a circle but as a decorative feature unlisted in the index, appeared in the composer's *The Singing-Master's Assistant* of 1778 and *Music in Miniature* of 1779; from the latter publication, too, come "Creation" and "Revelation," though both are expanded and the two upper parts of the first piece modified. Finally, the concluding section of the anthem "O Thou To Whom All Creatures Bow" stems from Billings' anthem "Peace" of c. 1783.[3]

The eight Lessons date back to 1778; they are a verbatim reprint (except for minor changes) of the larger part of the introduction in *The Singing-Master's Assistant*, which, in its turn, borrows most sentences in its two chapters on "Characters" from *Royal Melody Compleat* by the English composer William Tans'ur.[4] Lesson II in *The Continental Harmony* derives from Thomas Walter's *The Grounds and Rules of Musick Explained* (Boston, 1723, pp. 15–16).[5]

The theoretical introduction of *The Continental Harmony* was for the use of teachers of the singing-schools organized in the first part of the century in order to raise the musical standard of the divine service in New England churches. These schools had gradually developed into what we now call singing-societies, though marked by a devotion

[2] No author is mentioned for the three stanzas of "Connection." Whoever wrote them, possibly Billings himself, borrowed the words "Great is the Lord our God" from the opening of Watts's text that is associated with the 1778 edition of the music, and the words "Hail! Sacred Music" from the opening of the poem "On Musick," published in Billings' *The New-England Psalm-Singer* (1770).

[3] Pointed out by Ralph Th. Daniel, *The Anthem In New England Before 1800*, doctoral thesis, Harvard University, 1955, p. 190.

[4] From the 1767 Boston reprint of the 3rd London edition (see Irving Lowens, "The Origins Of The American Fuging Tune," *Journal Of The American Musicological Society*, VI, 1 [Spring 1953], 49). Billings forgot to add the heading "Lesson VII" in *The Continental Harmony*, p. 10, line 3.

[5] Also used in *The New-England Psalm-Singer*, chap. i; the jingle in *The Continental Harmony*, p. 25, appears here for the first time.

to an exclusively American repertoire of sacred music.

Billings devotes a great deal of space in his introduction (not merely in the Lessons but also in the appended Dialogue) to two topics: transposition and tonality. His ideas are quite simple, but they are couched in a terminology that needs explaining.

For the designation of the tones of our musical system he uses as many as three sets of symbols: (1) the traditional letters; (2) fa, sol, la (for C, D, E, and again for F, G, A) and mi (for the remaining tone B); (3) occasionally, the hexachord names of the Middle Ages and the Renaissance, such as G sol re ut and F fa ut. Two points must be kept in mind in reading Billings' statements: mi, B as well as B-mi, used interchangeably, constitute the seventh and frequently the "leading tone" in any major or minor scale and thus refer to a relative pitch; but, confusingly, B (or B-mi) also refers to a definite pitch, when it is, as the composer says, at its "native place." A sentence such as "Mi is in B, and now the question is where is B?" (p. 24) sounds like a riddle, and yet it is merely eighteenth-century jargon for warning the singer that the last interval in the major scale (and often in the minor scale as well) is a minor second. For example, if "B be flat, mi [the "leading tone" in what is now F major] is in E" (p. 4).

Billings attaches paramount importance to an understanding of the major and minor scales (with C major and A minor representing "the two natural primitive keys") without which, he believes, "No tune can be formed rightly or truly" (p. 11). Again his terminology differs from ours: he speaks of the "sharp" and the "flat" key. Passing up an opportunity to make an etymological point in commenting on the interval of the third in each (p. 21), he merely characterizes the minor sixth in the flat key as "a flat and melancholy sound" and the major sixth in the sharp key as "very martial and sprightly" (p. 27). Obsessed by the function of B, he further states (p. 26) that if it is below the "key note" (tonic), it indicates a sharp key (B-C in C major); if above, a flat key (A-B in A minor). Obviously his previous reference to B as "the sharpest tone in the whole octave"[6] would have added only confusion to this

[6] This happened when he attempted to explain (or rather to make pedagogically attractive) the circle of fifths (p. 24). Fancifully he calls F "the flattest tone in the whole octave." The "next sharpest" tones are E, A, etc., the next flattest C, G, etc. And then comes the catchy conclusion:" it is a maxim with musicians to flat the sharpest tones first, and sharp the flattest" (i.e., B flat in F major, E flat in B flat major, etc.; F sharp in G major, C sharp in D major, etc.).

sentence, and he wisely chooses not to repeat it. Since the flat key has a major seventh between its first and penultimate tone, though the latter is to be raised in cadences (p. 27), it is basically Aeolian — an archaic feature in the eighteenth century.

Sharp and flat keys, each unambiguous in psychological meaning, seem to him irreconcilable opposites. One is "sublime," "grand," "majestic"; the other "soft," "soothing," "pathetic" (p. 23), and he demands the strictest agreement between music and text, i.e., "flat keyed tunes [to be set] to melancholy words, and sharp keyed tunes to cheerful words" (p. 11); he regrets that he once made the mistake of composing a Hallelujah in a flat key (p. 22)[7]

Billings further makes distinctions between specific keys. He considers G minor as "more pensive and melancholy" than A minor, and he indeed confirms this in his music, at least with an appropriate choice of texts. On the other hand, his conviction that D major is "much more sprightly and expresses a shout better" than C major remains pure theory (p. 26).

From the introduction to *The Continental Harmony* we obtain valuable information about performance. There are first of all the so-called "moods." They function not merely as time signatures but, still largely obedient to the principle of the Renaissance tactus, they also indicate tempo. From the composer's detailed remarks (Lesson VI), we can construct the following table:[8]

Mood	Tempo	Mood	Tempo
⊂ Adagio	♩ = MM. 6σ	$\frac{3}{8}$	♩. = MM. 53
⊂ Largo	♩ = MM. 80		
⊃ Allegro	𝅗𝅥 = MM. 6σ	$\frac{6}{4}$	𝅗𝅥. = MM. 80
$\frac{2}{4}$	♩ = MM. 12σ		[MM. 60 in *The Singing-Master's Assistant*]
$\frac{3}{2}$	𝅗𝅥 = MM. 6σ		
$\frac{3}{4}$	♩ = MM. 80	$\frac{6}{8}$	♩. = MM. 80

Any one of these "moods" must be modified if "a quick,

[7] See the end of the anthem "Hear My Prayer O Lord" in *The New-England Psalm-Singer*. He should have also mentioned the Hallelujah and the preceding "cheerful" section in the anthem "Mourn, Mourn" in *The Continental Harmony*, pp. 149 to 151. It seems though that he merely forgot to add natural signs before "Be glad then America," since the melodic cadence that uses an F sharp (p. 150, score 2, m.1, counter) is applied only to his C major pieces and the $^6\!/_4$ type of the tenor melody in the Hallelujah (p. 151) always appears in C major also.

[8] Note Billings' consistent use of "minum" (half note) instead of "minim" (derived from "minima"). To judge by his previous publications, he knew better, but a few misprints in *The Singing-Master's Assistant* must have struck his fancy and persuaded him to indulge his sense of "originality" even in such a small detail as this one.

or slow term . . . [is] set over it," though this does not occur in *The Continental Harmony* except perhaps with such a marking as "Affettuoso." Billings then wants the tempo "one fourth part quicker or slower. . ." (pp. 20–21).

Not only were the "moods" and their English models (like Tans'ur) known to earlier American composers but also the specific hand motions with which the singers graphically described the metrical patterns and by which they learned them. Billings explains these motions in Lesson VI but does not consider them mere teaching aids. He demands an emphatically metrical rendition of his music (p. 28), with accents on 1 in triple time and on 1 and 3 in common time (even in fuging tunes, if the "air [apparently the accents of the initial motive] can be preserved"), and he believes he can reinforce the meter by appropriate manual gymnastics: "through the medium of the eye, as well as the ear . . . [the beating of time] conveys the accents into the minds of the audience, and serves to strike the passions in an extraordinary manner . . ." (p. 19).

From Billings' music alone one could not guess that it should be performed with precision in note values, coordination of the voices (p. 19), and tempo. Particularly the tempo in each "mood" had to be observed literally. The singers did this by guiding themselves by pendulums — home-made contraptions made of "common thread well waxed" and a small, round piece of wood which had been rubbed over with "chalk, paint or white-wash, so that . . . [it] may be seen plainly by candle light" (p. 7). Because of frequent tempo and meter changes in Billings' music, no doubt several pendulums — at least two for *The Continental Harmony* — had to be kept going at the same time.

There are but few dynamic indications. They are suggested by the "cheerful" or "melancholy" character of the text and the appropriate key. Volume is always straight; at only two places does it call for a "swell." Contrary to the concepts of polyphony, the entrance of each voice in fuging music is to be marked with increased strength[9] (p. 28).

Like his contemporaries, Billings uses ornamentation but

[9] See also *The Singing-Master's Assistant*, chap. xi: "and in performing *Pieces* where your part is sometimes silent [in a note Billings especially refers to "fuging Music"] . . . you must fall in with *spirit*; because that gives the Audience to understand another part is added, which perhaps they would not be so sensible of, if you struck in soft."

limits himself to the "grace of transition" (pp. 21 and 27–28). While he previously applied it to thirds, fourths, and, in cadences, even to major seconds, he now allows it only for thirds. The interval is to be filled in with a diatonic tone in the form of an eighth note, while a preceding half note becomes a dotted quarter. This he specifies in *The Singing-Master's Assistant* (p. 103), though in *The Continental Harmony* he merely says that the metrical accents should not be obscured. For this reason, too, he fears that where the notes that constitute the third, take up only a "half beat" (or, we may add, less than that), they, along with the grace, would sound like a triplet. In such cases and where the "mark of distinction" occurs, the notes should be left unornamented and made to sound "distinct and emphatic."

Women normally sang only the treble. The rest of the setting was for male voices, including the counter (the modern alto).[10] How many singers were assigned to each part Billings does not say, though in *The Singing-Master's Assistant* (pp. 14 and 15) he mentions a proportion of "three or four deep voices suitable for the Bass to one for the upper parts. . . ." Solo passages in anthems (at least according to *The New-England Psalm-Singer*, p. 18) are to be sung by two or three voices, and to sound "as Soft as an Echo. . . ."

It seems that the enthusiastic lay-member of New England singing-schools did not hesitate to choose any part that pleased him; he simply transferred it to a convenient register. Thus, the tenor and counter were occasionally sung an octave higher and the treble an octave lower.[11] Systematizing these possibilities in his own way, Billings suggests that the female treble double the tenor and the male tenor double the treble, i.e., an octave higher and lower respectively (pp. 15–16). This is preferably done simultaneously; otherwise, the second combination should be avoided.

[10] See pp. 4 and 5.

[11] *The New-England Psalm-Singer*, p. 21: "Treble . . . adapted to Feminine Voices in either Sex. . . ." (repeated in *The Singing-Master's Assistant*, p. 27); but Billings dislikes the male falsetto: "a Man cannot sing a proper Treble without counterfeiting a Woman's Voice, which is very unnatural, and in the Ears of most Judges very Disagreeable. . ." (*The New-England Psalm-Singer*, chap. ii). A report in the magazine *The Euterpiad* of Aug. 3, 1822 (quoted in Hamilton C. MacDougall, *Early New England Psalmody* [Brattleboro, Vt., 1940], p. 117), in mentioning anachronistic ways of singing in Massachusetts, refers to a female voice which doubles the counter in a high register (i.e., an octave higher).

The settings sound still fuller when Billings introduces "chusing notes" by dividing a voice part into two (p. 11). Either one may be sung but when both are heard "they add . . . to the variety." Appearing in the treble, the counter, and the bass (here usually at a distance of an octave, thus echoing the baroque effect of frequently doubled basses in *The New-England Psalm-Singer*), they often broaden a V-I cadence or lend sonority to a powerful image in the text. In passages for less than four voices or in "solos," it seems that their ad libitum character is no longer unrestricted.

Early American psalm-tunes were always notated with double bars marking the end of each line of the text. This indicated a brief rest; it also gave the deacon or clerk time for "lining-out," i.e., for reciting the next line so that it could be sung by the congregation. The practice was imported from late sixteenth-century England into the colonies and persisted into the eighteenth century. Billings inserts double bars only into his earliest publication, stating, in 1778,[12] that they are "but little esteemed among us." In *The Continental Harmony* (pp. 17–18) we learn that "lining-out" still existed in some New England churches. Billings rejects it emphatically as being "destructive to harmony" and to "the sense of the psalm."

Whether or not instrumental accompaniment was used cannot be decided categorically. It no doubt existed but it was entirely optional.[13] In *The New-England Psalm-Singer* (chap. ix) Billings says: "Let all Parts close in a proper Key, and a full Organ. . ."; and in *The Continental Harmony* (p. 14) he mentions an occasion when vocal pitch has to "conform to an instrument. . . ." However, his reference to the use of the "universally known" pitch-pipe (pp. 25 and 26) suggests an *a cappella* rendition. This seems to be confirmed, particularly for the present work, by Billings' enthusiasm about vocal music, whereas he considers instrumental music "but sound, and sound without sense",[14] and

[12] *The Singing-Master's Assistant*, p. 23.

[13] There are specific references to instruments in Billings' music only in two anthems. In "O Thou To Whom All Creatures Bow" in *The Continental Harmony*, the first of two textless passages is marked "Sym. to introduce B flat"; for this work, destined for ordination and therefore to be performed in church only, an organ was no doubt used. The other work which includes "symphonies" is "Peace." Here the term is defined as "sounds without words intended for Instruments," but in *The Singing-Master's Assistant*, p. 27, it is "an air, which is played, or sang [sic] without words, before the song begins, and sometimes such airs are in the middle of a peice [sic], and at the end."

[14] P. 15. This thought is even more forcibly expressed in an article "On Music" in *The American Magazine* (June 1788).

especially by his reference to the mutual doubling of treble and tenor as "sweet and ravishing, and . . . vastly preferable to any instrument whatever, framed by human invention" (p. 15).

For purposes of performance it may be useful to mention the following technical points: sections in the music that are to be repeated are enclosed by *:S:*; repetition of words is often indicated by :|:; a tie sometimes combines as many as three or four notes into one; the G clef of the tenor is to be read an octave lower; "b key" on page 86 (meaning "flat key") stands in the place of natural signs and thus changes E major to E minor; "Sharp key" on page 191 stands in the place of natural signs and changes G minor to G major.

Hardly any of Billings' ideas (or terminology) are novel. They are typical of their time. Nor can this be expected to be otherwise, since the purpose of the introduction was chiefly to set forth commonly recognized data. Nonetheless, all such introductions in American tune-books are of an extraordinary similarity in their wording, since they freely quote from each other, usually without acknowledgment (this was the age of plagiarism on both sides of the Atlantic), and occasionally from Tans'ur. It must not be assumed that Billings merely repeated what others said, for we know that he had read and given thought to contemporary theory and its application as published by the American Thomas Walter, and by Englishmen like Tans'ur,[15] John Arnold, Aaron Williams, and Joseph Stephenson.

Already in *The Singing-Master's Assistant* he had not contented himself with strait-laced textbook material but had lightened it with more fanciful writing. In *The Continental Harmony* he did the same by casting the greater part of his introduction into the form of a lively dialogue between master and scholar, a unique occurrence in American tune-books. Though it was probably suggested by *A New Musical Grammar* (first edition published in London in 1746) by William Tans'ur and *The Universal Psalmodist* (also published in London, first edition 1763) by Aaron Williams, it bears the unmistakable imprint of Billings'

[15] Billings (p. 30) erroneously speaks of Walker. His reference without doubt was to Walter's *The Grounds and Rules of Musick*, p. 24: "A Fourth is by some accounted a Chord, by others a Discord; but I am inclined to think the former." The statement on p. 16, line 16, refers to Tans'ur's *The Royal Melody Compleat*, chap. ii; lines 9 and 15, p. 17, are almost literal quotations from the same chapter.

personality. In turn he appears as the self-assured teacher and critic, eager to inform, and informing to the point of loquaciousness. He is the fervent and, in his own way, philosophizing preacher, and the chatty and clownish entertainer.[16] At his pleasure he resorts to any literary device at hand: solemn prose, jingling poetry, anecdotes, the homely phrase, and the contemporary catchword (in the form of military images). And he indulges in footnotes of every size and description, calling them "a glorious privilege, for which bad memories and dull authors cannot be too thankful" (p. 17). They also appear in the musical section of the book, several times to rectify what could have been decided before publication.[17] Thus the book (Billings admits to "broken hints and imperfect ideas" in his introduction, p. 33), has a dashing informality about it which distinguishes it from kindred volumes of its time.

The three types of music that Billings presents in *The Continental Harmony* are in form basically identical with those of contemporary tune-books. In the *psalm-tunes* the air is always carried by the tenor. Though marked by the composer's characteristic melodic style, it is traditional in its sparse use of melismas and its regard for the specific meter of its text,[18] thus also stressing the end of each or every other line. The four voices of the setting are rhythmically synchronized, now strictly, now slightly differentiated. Occasional rests within the tenor, which is ordinarily continuous, and florid passages as well as the appearance of contrasting "moods" within the same piece point to the influence of the anthem. The *fuging tune*, also related to the anthem, is based, like the previous type, on versified psalm-texts. It greatly appealed to Billings (p. 28); indeed, stimulated by English music, he was the first American composer to cultivate it.[19] It consists of two sections in

[16] The last line in "An Ejaculation of Philo Fuging," p. 28, had better be explained to the modern reader. Billings merely meant to say that the "hostilities" of rivaling voices will be resolved by an authentic cadence (see, for example, the two last chords in measures 4 and 5, score 1, p. 104, to which all of Billings' intervals apply, though he forgot to consider the lowest tone in the first chord).

[17] P. 42: the suggested transposition to a key a minor second lower is necessary, because the upper limit of the tenor range is exceeded. P. 117: the transposition "one note lower" (probably a major second) is necessary because the male counter rides too often on the C above middle C. The footnote on p. 48 refers to score 1, m. 4, which includes too many notes and faulty declamation of the words (the latter is common at this time); the passage can be rectified by shifting the third barline in this score one beat (the time of one half note) to the right.

[18] Chiefly Common Meter which consists of alternating 8- and 6-syllable lines.

[19] Lowens, "The American Fuging Tune," p. 44.

Scholar. Sir, if the ſcale of muſic was invented but about 700 years ago, how is it ſuppoſed the Royal Pſalmiſt, King David, and his celebrated choir of muſicians (both vocal and inſtrumental) performed by rule or rote?

Maſter. As it is not in my power to give a poſitive anſwer to your queſtion, perhaps it may not be a ſatisfactory one: but however it is rational to ſuppoſe, that King David and his choir, had the benefit of a certain rule or form, which was to them, both communicative and intelligible; and there is a paſſage in his life which both favours and ſtrengthens this ſuppoſition; you may find it recorded in the firſt book of Chronicles, 15th chap. and 22d verſe. *And Chenaniah, chief of the Levites, was for ſong; he inſtructed about the ſong, becauſe he was ſkilful.* I think this circumſtance amounts almoſt to a demonſtration; for it would be abſurd to ſuppoſe that Chenaniah ſhould be able to inſtruct ſo great a number, as we may reaſonably conjecture, or gather from ſcripture, would be under his immediate inſpection, or tuition, without a certain form or method, ſo as to make the performers exactly correſpond with each other both in time and ſound; therefore I think it is more than probable, that *Guido* by ſome means or other availed himſelf of King David's Scale,* and by making ſome few alterations and amendments, or it may be by climbing a few ſteps higher on a ladder of king David's raiſing, he (in ſpite of the royal author) has unjuſtly taken all the glory of the firſt invention to himſelf. But as this is a matter of mere conjecture, or dry ſpeculation, we muſt be content to leave it, where we found it, and proceed to ſomething more authentic.

Scholar. Sir, is it abſolutely neceſſary for B mi to be tranſpoſed ſo often as I ſee it i in your explanation? I think you ſay there are but *ſeven* letters, and yet there *fourteen* removes for B mi.

Maſter. Your remark upon that is very juſt; for as there are but ſeven letters, ſo there are but ſix removes, viz. B flat, B and E flat, B E and A flat, and F ſharp, F and C ſharp, and F C and G ſharp, theſe are the ſix removes for B mi, which, together with B mi natural, take up the ſeven letters; for if you add another flat, or ſharp, it will only be going over the ſame again; as for inſtance, if B E A and D be flat, mi is in G, which is the ſame as F C and

* I would not be underſtood, by the candid reader, to be guilty of ſo great a piece of abſurdity as this may appear to be, at the firſt glance; viz. the attempting to deſtroy a monument which (in the anſwer to the preceding queſtion) I was ſo induſtrious and ſolicitous in erecting, to immortalize the name of *Guido*; ſo far from that, I think I reflect great honour on *Guido*, in ſuppoſing him capable of improving, or making any addition to a muſical ſcale of King David's invention; the man who, in ſcripture, is ſtiled *The Lord's anointed, the man after God's own heart, the chief muſician,* &c. The daughters of Iſrael ſang by way of congratulation, "Saul hath ſlain his thouſands, and David his ten thouſands," and by way of ſimile, thus ſing I, "Guido hath done well, and David hath done better."

and G ſharp, ſo likewiſe if F C G and D be ſharp, mi is in D, which is the ſame as B E and A flat, ſo that after three removes by flats, and three by ſharps, the reſt are only a different way of expreſſing the ſame thing; therefore all the eſſential difference is in pitching the tune. Take this inſtance, ſuppoſe you have a ſharp key tune, with B and E flatted, ending on B; in order to make the voice conform to an inſtrument, you muſt not pitch the tune on B natural, but B flat; becauſe a flat inſerted at the beginning of the five lines ſerves to flat all notes that may happen on that line, or ſpace, unleſs it is contradicted by an accidental ſharp, or natural: and all ſharps that are placed at the beginning of the five lines, ſerve to ſharp all notes that may happen to be on that line, or ſpace, unleſs contradicted by an accidental flat, or natural; therefore in order to raiſe the tune, without removing the notes, you muſt take off the two flats, and ſubſtitute five ſharps; that is, F C G D and A muſt be ſharped, which bring Mi into the ſame place, and raiſes the tune a ſemitone higher; for B is now made natural; and if a tune ſtands too high, which is ſharped at the beginning, you may take off the ſharps, and ſubſtitute as many flats as will bring Mi into the ſame place; and in ſo doing, you will ſink the tune a ſemitone lower without removing the notes.

Scholar. Sir, I am obliged to you for being ſo explicit, and I doubt not but I ſhall reap the benefit of it; and now, ſir, if you pleaſe, we will proceed to the next thing in order, viz. the cliffs: pray ſir, why are they ſo called?

Maſter. The word cliff is much the ſame as a key, which ſerves to unlock, or let into a piece of muſic; for if there was no cliff marked you would be at a loſs to know how to begin, and you might ſuppoſe it to be either of the three cliffs, and you have two chances to gueſs wrong, where you have one to gueſs right.

Scholar. I ſee the neceſſity of them, pray, ſir, how many cliffs are in uſe, and what diſtance are they from each other?

Maſter. Three cliffs are as many as I ever knew, viz. the F, the C, and the G cliffs: The F cliff is the loweſt; the C cliff is a fifth higher than the F cliff; and the G cliff a fifth higher than the C cliff; unleſs the G cliff is ſet to the tenor, and then it is a fourth below the C cliff, and but one note above the F cliff.

Scholar. Are the cliffs always confined to one place?

Maſter. The F, and G cliffs are generally (and I believe always) confined, viz. the F cliff to the upper line but one in the baſs, and the G cliff to the lower line but one in the treble and tenor, but the C cliff is removed, from one

line

line to another, as the composer pleases, and Mr. *Williams* informs us that the cliff was formerly made use of to transpose B—Mi in the room of flats and sharps.

Scholar. Pray sir, what is the difference between the *Medius* and *Treble* ?

Master. When a piece of music is set in four parts, if a woman sings the upper part, it is called a *Treble*, because it is threefold, or the third octave from the Bass, but if a man sings it, it is called a *Medius*, or *Cantus*, because he sings it an octave below a Treble.

Scholar. Which is the best of these two ?

Master. It is sometimes set so, as for one part to be best, and sometimes the other ; but in general they are best sung together, viz. if a man sings it as a Medius, and a woman as a Treble, it is then in effect as two parts ; so likewise, if a man sing a Tenor with a masculine and a woman with a feminine voice, the Tenor is as full as two parts, and a tune so sung, (although it has but four parts) is in effect the same as six. Such a conjunction of masculine and feminine voices is beyond expression, sweet and ravishing, and is esteemed by all good judges to be vastly preferable to any instrument whatever, framed by human * invention.

Scholar. And is it a matter of indifference which part is sung, either *Medius*, or *Treble* ?

Master. No, for if one part must be omitted, I chuse it should be the Medius, because oftentimes notes in the Treble which are fifths above the Tenor, or Bass, when sung as a Medius, are converted into fourths below ; an instance

* We find it recorded in sacred writ, that "Jubal was the Father of all such as handled the harp and organ." But who was the father, or rather the former of the human voice ? *The Lord God Omnipotent* ! Then surely a greater than Jubal is here ; we know that neither Jubal, or any of his successors were ever able to frame an organ, that can distinctly articulate these words, "Hear my prayer O Lord," or change the key and say, "Praise the Lord O my soul," surely not. The most curious instrument that ever was constructed, is but sound, and sound without sense : while man, who is blest and endued with the faculties of speech can alternately sing of mercy and of judgment as duty bids, or occasion may require. The Royal Psalmist, who calls upon "every thing that hath breath to praise the Lord," has made this very beautiful distinction, where he says, "the *Singers* went *before*, the *Players* on *instruments* followed *after*." Here you see the singers took the lead, while the instrumental practitioners humbly followed after. *Lord what is man that thou hast thus distinguished him, for thou hast made him but a little lower than the angels, and hast crowned him with glory and honour.* To return, I think it no great encomium upon the Creator of heaven and earth, to acknowledge his superiority in constructing a vehicle for the conveyance of sounds, which is at once both capable of vociferation and articulation ; for indeed I think it not much short of blasphemy, to set up Jubal as a competitor with the Almighty of Heaven. Repent ye Jubalites, lest his jealousy awake and punish the presumption. "O Lord how manifold are thy works, in wisdom hast thou made them all." Help us O Lord to admire Jubal for thy sake, and adore thee for thine own sake. Then shall we render unto Jubal the things that are Jubal's, and unto God the things which are God's.

ſtance of which is in that admirable piece (compoſed by the ingenious Mr. Stephenſon) commonly known by the name of the 34th Pſalm: where the Tenor and Baſs begin in uniſon upon C, and the Treble on G Sol-re-ut line, which if ſung as a Treble is a fifth above the Tenor and Baſs, but if ſung as a Medius is a fourth below; and alſo notes which are thirds above, when ſung as a Treble, are converted into ſixes below, when ſung as a Medius, which fruſtrates the deſign of the compoſer; but when they are both ſung together, one ſerves to hide the imperfection of the other.

Scholar. Sir, I think you ſay that reſts are notes of ſilence, which ſignify that you muſt reſt or keep ſilence, as long as you would be ſounding one of the reſpective notes to which they belong; but it ſeems to me this rule does not hold good in a ſemibreve reſt, for in ſome moods of time, it contains more, and in ſome other, it contains leſs than a ſemibreve. I ſhould be glad if you would ſet that matter right.

Maſter. This would be more properly called a bar reſt, which is ſometimes longer, and ſometimes ſhorter, according to the variation of the time, for it will fill an empty bar in any mood of time; ſo that in $\frac{3}{2}$ it is half as long again as a ſemibreve, and in $\frac{2}{4}$ it is but juſt half as long as a ſemibreve; but for the future, I adviſe you to call it a bar reſt; becauſe it is not always a ſemibreve reſt, but in every mood of time, it is uſed as a bar reſt.

Scholar. Sir, I do not well underſtand the true intent of a *Hold*; for Mr. *Arnold* ſaith, that a note under a *Hold* muſt be holden ſomething longer than the time it contains, and Mr. *Tanſur*, does not ſay poſitively that it muſt, but that it may be holden longer than the note contains, if the performer pleaſe; he tells us that the French call it a *Surprize*.

Maſter. And in my opinion, it it very rightly named; for it is a matter of very great *ſurprize* to me, that any author ſhould give licenſe, and ſuch room for diſpute, as may (and to my certain knowledge does daily) ariſe from ſuch a paltry inſignificant thing; which is ſo far from being any benefit, that I have known a company of muſicians to break off in the middle of a piece, becauſe they were divided in ſentiment, at the occurrence of a *Hold*; ſome were for holding on the ſound ſomething longer than the time; ſome were for ſtopping to take breath, and perhaps in this party, no two would be agreed about the length of time they purpoſed to ſtop, but would begin one after another, as if they were performing a *Fuge*; others would be for going on without taking any notice of the *Hold*, which (in my opinion) is much the beſt way; for certainly if you hold on the note any longer than the time, it is impoſſible

ble to beat the *Bars* ; if the bar is full (as it ought to be) without it, there is no room for it, and if the bar be not full without it, certainly it is deficient with it ; and if any two ſhould diſpute upon it, there is authority for them to contradict each other ; for one may ſay he has a right to obſerve it, another will ſay he has a right to omit it, and both will refer each other to the ſame author, to prove what each one has aſſerted ; ſo that in fact they are both right, and yet diſagree at the ſame time ; therefore I think it ſo abſurd, that it is beſt to take no notice of it ; for my own part I never obſerve it, and I find upon enquiry that moſt judges of muſic are of my opinion.

Scholar. Sir, I have heard many diſpute about double Bars ; for ſome authors ſay that a double Bar dotted on each ſide ſignifies a Repeat ; and ſome ſay, that a double Bar without dots ſtands for a Repeat ; and others ſay you *may* ſtop at a double Bar, in pſalm tunes, the time of one or two beats, to take breath, *if* you pleaſe ; which ſometimes occaſions as much confuſion, as the occurrence of a Hold ; for if I am diſpoſed to ſtop, and another to proceed, I do not ſee how the time is to be preſerved.

Maſter. I do not ſee any more rule for ſtopping at a double Bar, than at a ſingle Bar, unleſs there be a reſt inſerted ; becauſe it cannot be done without loſing time ; and in my definition of a double Bar,* inſtead of ſaying, that you may ſtop to *take* breath, I ſhould have ſaid that you may ſtop to *catch* breath ; and even that muſt be done without loſing time ; but double Bars in Pſalm tunes are placed at the end of the lines, for the benefit of the ſight, to direct the performer, where to ſtop, in congregations where they keep up that abſurd † practice of reading between the lines, which is ſo deſtructive to harmony, and is a work of ſo much time, that unleſs the performers have very good

* I never place a double Bar for a repetition of notes, but always make uſe of an :S: though I ſometimes make uſe of a double Bar doted for a repetition of words ; for where the ſame word occurs ſeveral times ſucceſſively, a double bar doted anſwers the ſame purpoſe as the word written at length, and ſaves a great deal of labour and room.

† Among the many other abſurdities which always take place, where this contemptible practice of reading between the lines is ſtill kept up, this one may be added, viz. the great tendency it has to ſhut ſuch an excellent body of divine poetry (as is contained in the pſalm and hymn book now in vogue among us) out of private families ; for where the ſinging is carried on without reading, the performers muſt (of neceſſity) be furniſhed with books ; on the other hand, there are many who excuſe themſelves from procuring books in this manner, viz. why ſhould I be at this unneceſſary expenſe, when I am enabled (by the help of the Clerk, or Deacon) to ſing without it? Ironically, I anſwer, and why need we be at the expenſe of purchaſing a bible, or trouble ourſelves with peruſing it at home, ſo long as we may, by going to meeting once a week, hear a chapter or two gratis. (I confeſs this remark ſhould have been inſerted in the body of the work, but it did not take place in my mind till the pages were full ; therefore I plead benefit of *margin*, a glorious privilege, for which bad memories and dull authors cannot be too thankful.)

good memories, they are apt to forget the tune, while the line is reading. I defy the greateſt advocates for reading between the lines, to produce one word of ſcripture for it, and I will leave it to all judicious people, whether it is founded on reaſon; and certainly, whatever is founded on neither reaſon, nor religion, had better be omitted. The practice of retailing † the pſalm line by line, was introduced ſo long ago as when very few people had the knowledge of reading; therefore a reader was ſubſtituted for the whole congregation, who was called a Clerk; but at this time when every man is capable of reading for himſelf; and when we conſider the confuſion that is cauſed in the muſic, by reading the lines, and the deſtruction it occaſions to the ſenſe of the pſalm, I can ſee no reaſon for keeping up ſo abſurd a practice. Conſider further, that according to the practice in country churches, the pſalm is three times repeated. Firſt the miniſter reads it audibly alone, ſecondly the clerk, or deacon, line by line, and thirdly, it is ſung by the congregation; now if we are obliged to repeat the pſalm three times over, why are we not obliged to repeat our prayers as often before they would be deemed to be acceptable. I expect this doctrine will meet with ſome oppoſition in the country, but let who will concur or diſſent, I think myſelf highly honoured in having the approbation of the pious and learned Dr. WATTS* (that great maſter of divine ſong) who in his writings has declared himſelf to be of the ſame opinion.

Scholar. Sir, I ſhould be glad to know how many notes were formerly uſed when a ſemibreve was the ſhorteſt.

Maſter. The ancients made uſe of three other characters, viz. the *Large*, the *Long*, the *Breve*, and then the *Semibreve*; but the moderns have ſtruck out the three firſt, and ſubſtituted ſome leſſer notes, viz. the *Minum*, the *Crotchet*, the *Quaver*, &c. therefore the ſemibreve, which was formerly the ſhorteſt note, is (under the preſent ſyſtem) become the longeſt.

Scholar.

† Whatever Mr. Clerk, or Mr. Deacon, or Mr. Any-body-elſe, who ſuſtains the office of retailer may think; I ſhall take the liberty to tell them, I think it a very groſs affront upon the audience, for they ſtill go upon the old ſuppoſition, viz. the congregation in general cannot read; therefore they practically ſay, *we men of letters*, and *you ignorant creatures*.

* Here take the Doctor's own words. "It were to be wiſhed that all congregations and private families would ſing as they do in foreign proteſtant churches, without reading line by line, though the author has done what he could to make the ſenſe complete in every line or two, yet many inconveniences will always attend this unhappy manner of ſinging," &c. Thus he, the Rev. Doctor, does not tarry upon this ſubject long enough to enumerate the many inconveniences he ſeems to refer to. I imagine his reaſons for declining the taſk, were, the great tendency ſuch an undertaking would have to ſwell each page to a treatiſe, or rather a volume; therefore we may reaſonably conclude that the omiſſion was merely for want of room, not for want of reaſon.

Scholar. Sir, I want to know the difference between Common Time and Triple Time, and why one ſort of time is called Common and the other Triple Time?

Maſter. I believe your queſtion is but little underſtood; although it is very plain and eaſy, yet, through inattention, but few people entertain a right notion of it; for did mankind in general underſtand what is meant by *Time** in muſic, they would no longer entertain thoſe falſe ideas which they now do; viz. that common time is a very ſlow movement, and triple time a very quick movement. The eſſential difference between common time and triple time does not conſiſt in graveneſs or briſkneſs, but in the meaſure of the bars; for all moods in common time, are meaſured by even numbers, and all moods in triple time are meaſured by odd numbers, viz. by threes, for the very import of the word *Triple* is three-fold; therefore the moſt material difference between common time and triple time, is in accenting the bars, becauſe in common time the accent † falls twice in a bar, and in triple time but once. But to aſcertain the exact length of time in each particular mood, you muſt be governed by pendulums. But although triple time is differently barred from common time, yet all triple time moods are meaſured by the ſemibreve in common time, as thus: the firſt mood in triple time is called three to two; and now the queſtion which naturally ariſes, is this; why is it called three to two? Anſwer, becauſe each bar contains three minums, whereas a bar in common time contains but two, which is the length of one ſemibreve; therefore it is called three to two. The ſecond mood in triple time is called three from four, becauſe each bar contains three crotchets; whereas, a bar in common time contains four, which is the amount of one ſemibreve; therefore it is called three from four, becauſe it is taken from

* There are ſeveral ſpecies of good *Time*, which may be divided in the following manner, viz. one good diviſion of Time is, when the performers give each note its due proportion, viz. the ſemibreve as long again as the minum, the minum as long again as the crotchet, &c. Another good diviſion of time is, when the performers give each bar its due length of time, not performing one bar quicker than another. Another good diviſion of time is, when the performers move exactly together. Another good diviſion is, when the performers move in exact conformity to the vibration of a pendulum. N. B. Theſe are all grand diviſions, and to carry this military idea ſtill further, you may conſider the ſingle bars in the ſtead of file leaders, and the pendulum in the place of the ſtandard.

† You may take this as infallible, that your hand or foot muſt always be falling in the firſt part, or note in a bar, and riſing in the laſt part, both in common time and triple time. The motion of the hand in beating time is as correſpondent with the muſic, as the feet of the ſoldier is to the ſound of the fife; and through the medium of the eye, as well as the ear, it conveys the accents into the minds of the audience, and ſerves to ſtrike the paſſions in an extraordinary manner; for the accents are the life and ſpirit of the muſic, without which, it would be very inſipid, and deſtitute of meaning.

from four ſuch like notes in common time. The next mood in triple time is called three from eight, becauſe each bar contains three quavers, whereas a bar in common time contains eight, which is the amount of one ſemibreve; and in all moods of time, both in vocal and inſtrumental muſic, the ſemibreve is the meaſure note; therefore by obſerving the figures, you may tell how much is included in a bar, in any mood of time whatever, for the upper figure tells what quantity of notes is contained in a bar, but it does not tell what ſort of notes, whether they are minums, crotchets, quavers, or ſemiquavers; but the under figure tells how many notes of the ſame ſort is required to make one ſemibreve: Take this inſtance, ſuppoſe the time to be marked thus $\frac{6}{4}$, the upper figure ſignifies that there are ſix notes of ſome ſort included in each bar, and the under figure will determine them to be crotchets, becauſe four crotchets amount to one ſemibreve. N. B. You may depend upon the infallibility of this rule in any mood of time whatever.

Scholar. I think this is very plain; and now Sir, I want to know where to rank theſe moods of time called 6 to 4, and 6 from 8, whether in common or triple time?

Maſter. I think it is neither common time, nor triple time, but compoſed of both; yet it muſt be beat as common time, viz. three quavers down, and three up; for if you beat it as triple time, it is ſynonimous with three from four, there being the ſame quantity of notes included in a bar: but although the bars are filled in the ſame manner, yet there is as much difference between $\frac{3}{4}$ and $\frac{6}{8}$ as there is between any two moods whatſoever: for in $\frac{3}{4}$ the accent falls but once in a bar, in $\frac{6}{8}$ it falls twice in a bar; and it is impoſſible to beat $\frac{6}{8}$ as triple time without confounding the ſenſe of the time and tune: and if any are in doubt of the truth of this aſſertion, I adviſe them to try the experiment.

Scholar. If common time is meaſured by even numbers why is not $\frac{6}{8}$ entirely of the Binary ſpecies?

Maſter. This mood of time marked thus, $\frac{6}{8}$, ſimply conſidered, may be called common time, but in diſſecting the bar, the firſt diviſion falls out in threes, which makes it partake of the Trinary; the ſubdiviſion is likewiſe uneven, and that mood which will not bear dividing without partaking of the other ſpecies cannot properly be called either Binary, or Trinary, neither can it be ſaid to be neuter becauſe it partakes largely of the beauties of both.

Scholar. How much quicker, or ſlower, muſt a ſtrain be ſung for a quick, or ſlow term being ſet over it; for it ſeems to be a matter of uncertainty and ſometimes occaſions a great deal of diſpute?

Maſter.

Maſter. I dont know what other authors may intend, but I ſhould be glad to have ſuch ſtrains, performed one fourth part quicker or ſlower ; for if it is not reduced to a matter of certainty, it may occaſion not only a great deal of diſpute but alſo a great deal of confuſion, and moſt practitioners who are not thorough maſters of time, are very apt to drive the time, eſpecially in the Allegro mood.

Scholar. Sir, I ſhould be glad to know whether the grace of tranſition ſhould be always uſed in tuning thirds up and down ?

Maſter. Where the time of the notes will admit of it, I am very fond of the notes being graced by ſounding the intermediate note, which ſerves for a ſtair for the performer to ſtep up or down upon ; but where the notes are but a half beat in length, you muſt not ſtrike the intermediate note, becauſe the two outſide notes are ſo ſhort, that if you ſpend any time upon the intermediate note, it makes them ſound like notes tied together, in threes, which is very falſe, and entirely ſpoils the *air* ; but where you meet with ſuch notes, you muſt ſtrike them as diſtinct and emphatic as if a mark of diſtinction was placed over their heads.

Scholar. Sir, I want to know the eſſential difference between a flat key, and a ſharp key ?

Maſter. You will find that the third above the flat key, contains but three ſemitones, and the third above the ſharp key, contains four ſemitones.*

Scholar. Sir, I ſhould be glad to know which key you think is beſt ; the flat, or the ſharp key ?

Maſter. I believe your queſtion would puzzle the greateſt philoſopher, or practitioner, upon earth ; for there are ſo many excellent pieces on each key, that we are apt to fall in with a certain man, who heard two very eminent lawyers plead in oppoſition to each other ; after the firſt had done ſpeaking, the man was ſo charmed with his eloquence and oratory, that he thought it would be an idle (as well as a raſh) attempt for any one to gainſay, or contradict him ; but when he had heard the ſecond, he ſaid, that his reaſons were ſo nervous and weighty, he was about to give him the preference ; upon which the firſt made ſo forcible a reply, that the man knew not what to ſay, at laſt he concluded they were both beſt. Similar to this, let us ſuppoſe ourſelves to be auditors to a company of muſicians ;

* To the above definition this might be added, viz. that the flat key has its leſſer *ſixth*, and *ſeventh*, riſing above the key note ; and the ſharp key has its greater *ſixth* and *ſeventh*, riſing above the key note ; but as theſe are circumſtances which muſt take place in conſequence of the former, they are ſuppoſ- to be included in the above anſwer.

cians: how enraptured ſhould we be to hear the ſharp key, expreſs itſelf in ſuch lofty and májeſtic ſtrains as theſe! *O come let us ſing unto the Lord, let us make a joyful noiſe, to the rock of our ſalvation; let us come before his preſence with thankſgiving, and make a joyful noiſe unto him with pſalms. Sing unto the Lord all the earth, make a loud noiſe, rejoice and ſing praiſe!* Do I hear the voice of men, or angels! ſurely ſuch angelic ſounds cannot proceed from the mouths of ſinful mortals: but while we are yet warm with the thought, and raviſhed with the ſound, the muſicians change their tone, and the flat * key utters itſelf in ſtrains ſo moving, and pathetic, that it ſeems at leaſt to command our attention to ſuch mournful ſounds as theſe: *Hear my prayer O Lord, give ear to my ſupplication, hear me ſpeedily: O Lord my ſpirit faileth, hide not thy face from me; O my God, my ſoul is caſt down within me. Have pity upon me, O ye my friends, for the hand of God hath touched me.* O how theſe ſounds thrill through my ſoul! how agreeably they affect my nerves! how ſoft, how ſweet, how ſoothing! methinks theſe ſounds are more expreſſive than the other, for they affect us both with pleaſure and pain, but the *pleaſure* is ſo great it makes even *pain* to be pleaſant, ſo that for the ſake of the pleaſure, I could forever bear that pain. But hark! what ſhout is that? It ſeems the ſharp key is again upon the wing towards heaven; jealous, perhaps, that we pay too much deference to his rival: he not only deſires, but *commands* us to join in ſuch exalted ſtrains at theſe. *Rejoice in the Lord, and again I ſay, rejoice, O clap your hands all ye people, ſhout unto God with the voice of triumph; God is gone up with a ſhout, the Lord with the ſound of a trumpet; ſing praiſes to God, ſing praiſes, ſing praiſes unto our King, ſing praiſes.* What an ecſtacy of joy may we ſuppoſe the Royal Author to be in when he compoſed this Pſalm of praiſe! perhaps it might be ſome ſuch ſtrain as this, that expelled the evil ſpirit, and I wiſh it might expel ſome of the *evil ſpirits* in theſe days, who are averſe to hearing God's praiſes ſung, in ſuch a manner as the Pſalmiſt has here pointed out: but I would refer ſuch perſons to King David, for their character, who ſays, *they are like the deaf adder, who ſtoppeth her ear, and will not hearken to the voice of charmers, charming never ſo wiſely.* But to return, you ſee the extreme difficulty, and almoſt impoſſibility of giving the preference to either of theſe keys, both of which are ſo agreeable to our natures, and are ſo excellent

that

* I take this opportunity to make this remark, viz. the impropriety of ſetting a *Hallelujah* in a flat key; the reader may obſerve, that the import of the word is, *Praiſe ye the Lord.*—Query, is it not very inconſiſtent to praiſe the Lord, in tones which are plaintive and prayerful? for certainly the words and the muſic, muſt contradict each other. N. B. This errour I confeſs myſelf guilty of in a former publication, but upon more mature reflection, I heartily wiſh it were in my power to eraſe it.

that they ſeem to excel each other ; * for when we are juſt about to declare ourſelves in favour of one, the other comes and pleads its own cauſe ſo powerfully upon our nerves, that it not only ſtaggers, but ſometimes ſets us quite beſide our purpoſe ; for the one is ſo ſublime, ſo grand, and ſo majeſtic, † the other, ſo ſoft, ſo ſoothing, ſo pathetic ; in fact, the key which comes laſt ſeems to be the beſt, and generally leaves the greateſt impreſſion. Hiſtory gives us an account very ſimilar to this in the Life of Alexander the Great, viz. that while he was ſitting at table (calmly and quietly) his muſician would ſtrike upon a majeſtic ſtrain on the ſharp key, ſounding *to arms, to arms, to arms*, in ſuch animating and commanding ſounds, that the king being filled with martial rage, would ſtart from table, draw his ſword, and be juſt about to ſally forth, in order to ſlay his enemies, when none were near him ; but even while martial fury had the aſcendency over reaſon, the muſicians would change the key, and play ſuch moving and melting airs ; viz. *Darius is fall'n, fall'n, fall'n*, that the king (being melted into pity) would let his ſword drop out of his hand, ſit down and weep heartily for him, whoſe deſtruction he had been always ſeeking, and whoſe ruin he had but juſt accompliſhed. For my own curioſity I have been very critical in my obſervations, and very induſtrious in my inquiries, and I find that moſt men who are lovers of muſic, are affected in the ſame manner (though not often to ſuch a degree) as Alexander was ; but at the ſame time, if all, who are lovers of muſic, were to decide the point by vote, I am poſitive the flat key would have the preference by a great majority.

Scholar. Sir, I do not well underſtand you, for you have but juſt given it as your opinion, that the two keys, were to moſt men equally pleaſing ; therefore I ſhould be glad to hear you explain yourſelf further.

Maſter. When I ſpoke in that manner, I meant to confine the obſervation to the male ſex : but you may take it for granted, that the female part of the creation are much the greateſt lovers of muſic ; for I ſcarcely ever met with one but what was more or leſs entertained with muſical ſounds, and I am very poſitive that nine tenths of them

are

* It is probable that at the firſt glance, this may appear inconſiſtent, viz. that any two things oppoſed ſhould be ſaid to excel each other ; but I preſume (upon ſecond thought) all who are judges of muſic will allow that the ſharp and the flat key are ſo excellent each in its own way, that conſidering them in this light, though ſo different, they may (without any impropriety) be ſaid to excel each other.

† I think it may not be amiſs to rank the ſharp key (by reaſon of its majeſty and grandeur) in the maſculine, and flat key (by reaſon of its ſoftneſs and effeminacy) in the femenine gender ; and all indifferent pieces, which are of no force in either key, may (with contempt) be ranked in the neuter.

are much more pleaſed and entertained with a flat, than a ſharp air ; and I make no doubt, but that the muſical world (if upon reading what I have now aſſerted, they ſhould be induced to make ſome obſervations that way) muſt unavoidably fall into my opinion.

Scholar. Sir, I dont well underſtand the tranſpoſition of keys, or the removal of B-mi from one place to another; I ſhould be glad to have it explained.

Maſter. In the firſt place, Mi is in B, and now the queſtion is, where is B ? and that you muſt find out by the cliffs ; and you will find it to be the next letter but two above the F cliff, the next letter below the C cliff, and the next letter but one above the G cliff ; ſo that for inſtance, ſuppoſe the G cliff, to be on the lower line but one, then B-mi is on the middle line, and in that caſe you muſt always ſuppoſe it to be there ; but if there is a flat * ſet on B, it removes it to E ; that is, B is then where E was, when B was on the middle line ; and E is removed into the place of ſome other letter in order to make room for B ; for when B removes, all the other letters muſt move with it, like ſo many attendants ; ſo that when B is in the place of E, C being always one letter higher, muſt conſequently be in the place of F, and A being one letter below, B muſt be in the place of D ; ſo that you ſee by placing a flat on B the whole ſcale is removed either a fourth higher than what it was before ; or a fifth below. The next remove is effected by adding another flat, and that muſt be put on the place where B-mi is, viz. on E, and that removes B into the place of A, and in order to make room for B, A modeſtly ſteps down into the place of G ; and here you ſee the remove is either a fourth above, or a fifth below : the next remove is by placing another flat on A, and that removes B into the place of D, and this remove is either a fourth above, or fifth below ; ſo you ſee placing a flat on the place where B ſtands, always removes it either a fourth above, or a fifth below. The next remove is by placing a ſharp on F, which draws B out of its native place into its own place, which removes it either a fifth above, or a fourth below ; the next remove is made by placing a ſharp on C, which draws B out of F into C, and this remove is either a fifth above, or fourth below ; the next remove is made by placing a ſharp on G, which draws B out of C into G, and this remove is either a fifth above, or a fourth below : theſe are all the removes of B-mi : and I would have you obſerve,

that

* The reaſon why B is the firſt letter flatted, is, becauſe it is the ſharpeſt tone in the whole octave, and E is the next ſharpeſt tone, and A the next, and ſo on as they are laid down in the rules of tranſpoſition : and the reaſon why F is firſt ſharped, is, becauſe it is the flatteſt tone in the whole octave, C is the next, G is the next, &c. For it is a maxim with muſicians to flat the ſharpeſt tones firſt, and ſharp the flatteſt.

that by inserting a flat you drive B either a *fourth* higher, or a *fifth* lower; whereas by inserting a sharp, it is just the contrary, for that draws B either a *fifth* higher, or a *fourth* lower; and I would have you take notice that flats drive B out of any letter, and sharps draw it into any letter; for instance, suppose B to be on the middle line, then by placing a flat on the middle line, you drive B into E, then by placing a flat on E, you drive B into A, then by placing a flat on A, you drive A into D; on the other hand, by placing a sharp on F, you draw B into F, then by placing a sharp on C, you drive B into C, then by placing a sharp on G, you draw B into G; so you see the last sharp always carries B with it, whereas the last flat always drives B from it; and that is the reason why flats are said to drive, and sharps to draw. The Poet expresses it thus:

"By flats the *mi* is driven round,
"Till forc'd on B to stand its ground.
"By sharps the *mi's* led through the keys,
"Till brought *home* to its *native* place."

You must likewise remember that where Mi is, there is B; for fa, sol, la, mi, are only other names for the letters, but when you pitch a tune by a pitch pipe, you must draw out the pipe to the key note, without paying any regard to transposition, that is, if the key note stands upon the G-sol-re-ut line although G is removed to some other place, by the transposition of B-mi, yet it is always considered as in its native place on a pitch pipe, and so are all the other letters, unless there is a flat or sharp set on the letter the tune is pitched on, which raises it, or lowers it a semitone; thus you see, that no tune can end on any other letter but C, or A, for when B-mi is removed to any other place in the scale, A is always the next letter under it, and C, the next letter above it; and I have told you elsewhere that your tune must always end one note above, or one note below B-mi, which brings the key always into C or A.

Scholar. Sir, I do not see the necessity of transposing B-mi from one place to another, for if the tune must always end on A or C, I do not see any great difference between a tune that is set in its native place and one that is transposed, and I am sure it would be much easier for the learner if it was always confined to one place.

Master. The transposing of B-mi oftentimes serves to keep the tune more in the compass of the five lines, than it could possibly be, if B-mi stood in its native place, and likewise gives a variety of airs. For any one who is acquainted

quainted with mufic will allow that a fharp key tune ending on D, is much more fprightly and expreffes a fhout better than one which ftands on C ; fo likewife, a flat key tune ending on G is more penfive and melancholy, than one which ftands on A, and every letter has its own peculiar air, which air is very much hurt if the tune is not rightly pitched ; for inftance, if a tune is fet on A natural, and in pitching the tune, you fet it a tone too low, you tranfpofe the key into G, which is perhaps quite different from the intention of the author, and oftentimes very deftructive to the harmony, for there is a certain pitch for every tune where it will go fmoother and pleafanter than it would on any other letter whatfoever.

Scholar. Sir, I think I have read in fome authors, that if the performers can found the higheft and loweft note in a tune clear, the tune may be faid to be well pitched.

Mafter. There is no general rule without fome exceptions, and I think in this rule there is room for a very great one, for perhaps in a company of fingers, one may be able to ftrike feveral notes above G-fol-re-ut in Alt, another perhaps can ftrike double B in the Bafs ; now can that tune always be faid to be well pitched, becaufe thefe two extraordinary voices can ftrike the two extreme notes ? fo far from it, that by this rule there is room to pitch the tune perhaps five or fix notes too high, or too low.

Scholar. Sir, I fhould be glad to know what rule I am to be governed by in this cafe.

Mafter. The beft general rule I know of, is, to fet the tune on the * letter the author has fet it, unlefs he has given directions to the contrary ; for it is to be fuppofed that any one, who has fkill enough to compofe a piece of mufic, has likewife judgment enough to fet it on a proper key. But although this rule is good in general, yet it is not infallible ; for oftentimes the greateft mafters of compofition fet fome of their pieces too high or too low, which you will foon difcover by making yourfelf mafter of the tune.

Scholar. Sir, I want to know if there are not fome principal or dominant tones befides the key note which ferve to regulate the reft ?

Mafter. In the firft place, you muft pay great attention to the *key note*, and the found of B-mi which conftitutes the key note, and caufes it to be either flat or † fharp ; the next principal tone to be regarded, is the *third* above the

key

* The utility of that little inftrument, called a *Pitch Pipe*, is fo univerfally known and acknowledged, that it would be needlefs for me to engrofs the reader's time in proving a thing which is already granted.

† It may not be amifs here to trace this matter back to the fountain head, viz. the *cliffs*, for the *cliffs* afcertain the place of B-mi, and B-mi conftitutes the *key note*, and that determines the *tones* above or below it to be either flat or fharp, according to the fcale.

key note, which contains a great part of the true air of the tune, for by the ſound of the *third*, we are enabled to tell whether the key is flat or ſharp ; another principal tone is the *ſixth* above the key note, which is either flat or ſharp, according to the key of the tune ; for the *ſixth* above A, the natural flat key, contains but eight ſemitones, viz. from A to F, which is a flat and melancholy ſound ; whereas the *ſixth* above C, the natural ſharp key, contains nine ſemitones, viz. from C to A, which is very martial and ſprightly, and I think is almoſt as great a mark of diſtinction as the *third* · the *ſeventh* is likewiſe a guide in this caſe, for the *ſeventh* above the flat key contains but ten ſemitones, whereas the *ſeventh* above the ſharp key contains eleven ſemitones. The *fourth* is no guide in this caſe, for there are the ſame number of ſemitones included in the *fourth* above the flat key as there is above the ſharp, viz. from A to D is five ſemitones, and from C to F is five ſemitones : the *fifth* is no guide in this caſe, for the ſame number of ſemitones are included in the fifth above the flat, as there are above the ſharp key, viz. from A to E is ſeven ſemitones, and from C to G is ſeven ſemitones : the *octave* is no guide at all in this caſe, for every *octave* contains twelve ſemitones.

N. B. Experience will teach you that great advantages will ariſe from theſe obſervations.

Scholar. Sir, I have obſerved in a ſharp key tune, moſt people are apt to ſtrike B-mi too ſharp, ſo as to make but little diſtinction between B-mi and C-fa ; can you render any reaſon for it ?

Maſter. I believe it is the power of attraction in the key note, which is naturally very drawing. A proof of this you may obſerve in a flat key tune, where the note before the cloſe ſtands on G ſol, which is a whole tone below the key ; but it is ſo natural to ſharp it, that it ſeems to be doing violence to nature to ſtrike it without the ſharp ; and I preſume all maſters of muſic, both vocal and inſtrumental, will allow this to be fact, and as a further proof of what I have aſſerted, you may obſerve that B-mi is eaſy to ſtrike in a flat key, and ſo is G-ſol, in a ſharp key.

Scholar. Sir, I have obſerved that ſtrangers who are well ſkilled in the rules of muſic, do not harmonize ſo well at firſt trial, as thoſe who are better acquainted with each others voices ; I cannot conceive the reaſon, for I always thought the rule was ſo extenſive and infallible as to cauſe as much harmony between thoſe who never ſung together before, as between thoſe who were intimately acquainted with each others voices.

Maſter. Strangers often diſagree about the grace of tranſition, or ſliding from one note to another, eſpecially in turning thirds, for ſome will lean very hard upon the intermediate note, and ſome will not touch it at all, but will leap

leap from one note to another as they would in a fourth, or any other diftance; but they oftener difagree about the emphatical notes in the tune, for fome authors confine the emphatical or accented notes to the firft part of the bar, both in common and triple time, and fome lay the emphafis on the firft and third parts of the bar, in common time, and fome others let them fall where they may happen, without any reftraint at all; but it is much the beft way (I think) to lay the emphafis on the firft part of the bar in triple time, and on the firft and third parts of the bar in common time, though fometimes it is very difficult for the compofer to accent the bars without lofing the air, efpecially in fuging mufic;* but if the air can be preferved, and the bars properly accented alfo, it difcovers much more ingenuity in the compofer, and adds a greater luftre to the compofition, and it would likewife have a tendency

to

* It is an old maxim, and I think a very juft one, viz. *that variety is always pleafing*, and it is well known that there is more variety in one piece of fuging mufic, than in twenty pieces of plain fong, for while the tones do moft fweetly coincide and agree, the words are feemingly engaged in a mufical warfare; and excufe the paradox if I further add, that each part feems determined by dint of harmony and ftrength of accent, to drown his competitor in an ocean of harmony, and while each part is thus mutually ftriving for maftery, and fweetly contending for victory, the audience are moft luxurioufly entertained, and exceedingly delighted; in the mean time, their minds are furprizingly agitated, and extremely fluctuated; fometimes declaring in favour of one part, and fometimes another.—Now the folemn bafs demands their attention, now the manly tenor, now the lofty counter, now the volatile treble, now here, now there, now here again.—O inchanting! O ecftatic! Pufh on, pufh on ye fons of harmony, and

Difcharge your deep mouth'd canon, full fraught with Diapafons;
May you with Maeftofo, rufh on to Choro-Grando,
And then with Vigorofo, let fly your Diapentes
About our nervous fyftem.

An Ejaculation of Philo Fuging.

Grant I befeech thee, O Apollo, that thefe thy devotees may never want competitors, and let thefe thy fugers be unanimoufly difagreed, and fweetly irreconcilable.—

Hark! Hark! hear the voice of reafon, who in difguife has attended through the whole controverfy, and thus fhe addreffes the contending parties. "Give over your fruitlefs endeavours, ye fons of Confonance, and no longer attempt impoffibilities, for we have heard with our ears, and our auditory nerves have informed us, that the author of this compofition has ingenioufly turned all your efforts for afcendency into the right channel, fo that all your extraordinary exertions for fupremacy, has but a tendency to animate and ftimulate your rival competitors; therefore we do, by and with the advice of the author, both counfel and command that (for the prefent) you let all mufical hoftilities fubfide, and it is our royal will and pleafure, that your thirds and fourths, your fixths and tenths, be refolved into the unifon and octave, the twelfth and fifteenth from the bafs.

By the command of REASON,

The Author, Secretary.

to bring ftrangers to a better agreement about ufing Forte and Piano, fo that one voice would not be fo apt to fwallow up the other, as is fometimes the cafe, when they are at a lofs about accenting.*

Scholar.

* But fays the critic. Ah! well, what fays the critic? "I think, Mr. Author, your *precept* is excellent, and your *practice* but indifferent, for in your New England Pfalm Singer, you feem to take but little notice of either *emphafis* or *accent*, and whether the reafon is founded either upon ignorance or inattention, I am not able to determine, but I am rather inclined to think the former." Hark you, Mr. Critic, a word in your ear, hear and be aftonifhed, and let me affure you, upon the word and honour of an author, that what I am about to confefs is neither ambiguous nor ironical, but you may depend upon my fincerity, when I acknowledge, I was fool enough to commence author before I really underftood either *tune*, *time*, or *concord*. "Indeed, this from your heart." This from my very foul. "Amazing, what condefcenfion is this, in an author of your popularity? But fure, Mr. Author, you do not intend to publifh this acknowledgement to the world." O, by no means, as I told you before, this is only a word in your ear. "But if my opticks inform me right, I faw this fame confeffion inferted, verbatim, in a dialogue between you and your pupil, how then do you fuppofe it poffible to conceal it from the world, when it is typically conveyed to every reader." Softly Sir, not quite fo loud, if my pupil (who is hard by) fhould chance to hear your interrogation or my confeffion, his great opinion of my infallibility, would be entirely deftroyed, and inftead of refpect for my knowledge, he would, no doubt, fhow his contempt of my ignorance, and he might alfo (with great propriety) exprefs his indignation at my impudence in attempting to inftruct him in a fcience of which I have confeffed myfelf entirely ignorant; although fuch teachers are no *novelty*, yet no doubt the confequences to me would be this; the lofs of my character, which would be attended with the lofs of my bufinefs, and confequently the lofs of my bread; therefore Sir, in the name of charity, I muft entreat you not to be fo clamorous. "But indeed, Mr. Author, your manner of anfwering my laft queftion is very foreign from the purpofe, and entirely evafive; but I am refolved your equivocation fhall not excufe you from anfwering this concife queftion. How do you expect to keep private, what you have already made public?" I do not intend to have it inferted in the body of the work, but by way of whifper in a marginal note, and I intend to order the printer to print it on a very fmall type, in an obfcure part of the book, and as near the bottom of the page as poffible. I fuppofe, Mr. Critic, I need not inform you that all readers may be divided into thefe two claffes, viz. the *curious* and *incurious*; the curious reader, by perufing this work, will (without this information of mine) be fully fatisfied that the compofition is both inaccurate and indifferent; therefore, as I tell him no more than he knew before, my popularity will not be diminifhed by this frank confeffion; but if he has a fpark of generofity, he will beftow large encomiums both on my honefty and modefty; and if he does not (I ftill further confefs) I fhall be prodigioufly chagrined, and confoundedly difappointed. As to the incurious readers (by way of gratitude) I confefs they are a fet of people I have a great refpect for; becaufe they conftitute the greater part of my admirers; and as they feldom trouble themfelves with marginal notes (unlefs fome Type-Mafter-General fhould be fo illnatured as to inform againft me) they would be none the wifer, and (by this artful evafion) I prefume I fhall be none the worfe for this honeft declaration And now Sir, in my turn, I fhall take it upon me (however you may receive it) to interrogate you. Pray Sir, how came you fo impertinently officious in your criticifms upon me? You fyllable catcher, if you are but half fo honeft as I am condefcending, you will acknowledge I *have made game out of your own hand*, and beat you at your own weapons! You comma hunter, did I not inform you that I intended to difcharge you from my fervice, and do my own drudgery; and now Mr. Semi-critic, once more I command you to quit my Confonance, with the velocity of a Demifemi; and

If you ever be fo hardy as to traverfe my Quartas,
Or fcore off your Eptachords with my Diapafons,
I folemnly proteft,

By

Scholar. Sir, I want to know your opinion of a fourth, for as ſome call it a concord, and ſome a diſcord, and as I have obſerved it to be very much uſed in compoſition, I am at a loſs where to rank it.

Maſter. I think Mr. *Walker* is the only author I ever read, who is ſo fond of a fourth, as to call it a concord, for a fourth, ſimply conſidered, without diſpute is a diſcord * (at leaſt to my ear) though not ſo harſh and diſagreeable as a ſecond or a ſeventh, for the harſh ſound of a fourth may be ſo mollified and ſweetened by a fifth and an eighth, as to induce thoſe, who are led more by the ear than by the underſtanding, to think that the three ſounds were all perfect concords to each other ; for inſtance, let one note ſtruck on the F faut cliff in the baſs, another on C faut in the tenor, which is a fifth from the baſs, and another on F faut in the counter, which is an eighth from the baſs, and a fourth from the tenor, theſe three ſounds harmonize almoſt as well as any three ſounds in nature ; but if you take away the baſs you mar all the muſic, becauſe in taking away the baſs† you take off the fifth and the eighth, which is produced

By the graveneſs of Adagio, and vivacity of Allegro,
The Forte of my Canon well charg'd with Septi Nonas,
Shall greet your Auditory with terrible Senſations,
And fill you with tremor.
I'll beat your empty bars in the twinkle of a pendulum,
By way of Syncopation I'll ſcore your compoſition,
And with a ſingle Solo I'll cloſe up your Chorus
In tacitneſs eternal.

* Although it is generally ſuppoſed by philoſophers that the more frequent the coincidences the more agreeable the concord, yet Mr. Martin (in his Philoſophical Grammar) ſays, " there is ſomething elſe beſides the frequency of coincidences, which conſtitute a concord," otherwiſe a fourth would have the preference to a greater third, which is contrary to experience.

† The utility of the baſs is as conſpicuous in this example, as it can poſſibly be, for by taking away one note you take away two concords, which were not only concords in themſelves, but by their joint force they converted a diſcord into a concord ; and in order to illuſtrate this point ſtill more fully, you may ſelect out one of the beſt tunes that was ever compoſed, and let the upper parts perform without the baſs, the noiſe would be almoſt intolerable, but, vice verſa, let one of the upper parts be taken off and the baſs ſubſtituted in its ſtead, the concert would be agreeable, although it would be diminiſhed from a full chorus. And here it may not be amiſs to inform the reader that in a concert of four parts, with their octaves, there is a great number of chords, or harmonious tones ſtruck at the ſame time ; I have heard between twenty and thirty different tones ſtruck from the four parts, and their octaves ; but time would fail me to inſiſt largely upon this ſubject, for if a man (Briarious like) had a hundred hands, and a pen in each hand, the ages of all men from Adam down to the preſent day, multiplied together, would be too little to comment at large upon this ſubject, and I think I may ſafely defy all the mathematicians in the univerſe, to calculate the number of coincidences and vibrations which take place at one and the ſame inſtant of time, for there is ſomething magical in it, and out of the reach of human art. Dr. Biles expreſſes it very beautifully and emphatically in the following Lines,

" Then rolls the rapture through the air around,
" In the full magic melody of ſound."

produced by the baſs and tenor, and baſs and counter, and leave only the fourth, which is produced by the tenor and counter, and I would adviſe thoſe perſons who are ſo fond of a fourth, to try this method, and if, after that, they ſtill continue of the ſame mind, I ſhall be induced to think that one ſound is almoſt as agreeable to them as another.

Scholar. Sir, I ſhould be glad to know whether you have any particular rule for introducing diſcords, in muſical compoſition; I think you ſay that you have not tied yourſelf to any rules laid down by others, and I want to know whether you have formed a ſet of rules in your own mind, by which you are governed in ſome meaſure.

Maſter. Muſical compoſition is a ſort of ſomething, which is much better felt than deſcribed, (at leaſt by me) for if I was to attempt it, I ſhould not know where to begin or where to leave off; therefore conſidering myſelf ſo unable to perform it, I ſhall not undertake the taſk; but in anſwer to your queſtion, although I am not confined to rules preſcribed by others, yet I come as near as I poſſibly can to a ſet of rules which I have carved out for myſelf; but when fancy gets upon the wing, ſhe ſeems to deſpiſe all form, and ſcorns to be confined or limited by any formal preſcriptions whatſoever; for the firſt part is nothing more than a flight of fancy, the other parts are forced to comply and conform to that, by partaking of the ſame air, or, at leaſt, as much of it as they can get: But by reaſon of this reſtraint, the laſt parts are ſeldom ſo good as the firſt; for the ſecond part is ſubſervient to the firſt, the third part muſt conform to firſt and ſecond, and the fourth part muſt conform to the other three; therefore the grand difficulty in compoſition, is to preſerve the air through each part ſeparately, and yet cauſe them to harmonize with each other at the ſame time.

Scholar. Which of the concords is moſt uſeful in compoſition?

Maſter. I believe the third is the moſt in uſe of any concord in nature, for it ſeldom comes amiſs; the ſixth is alſo in great requeſt, but it does not ſo often take place between the tenor and baſs, as between the tenor and counter, tenor and treble, counter and treble, &c. But in my opinion the octave to a greater third, viz. a tenth, is the grandeſt concord in nature; the fifth is by far the ſweeteſt, but not ſo durable as the tenth, becauſe it is ſo luſcious and fulſome that it is apt to cloy, and that I ſuppoſe to be one reaſon which forbids two of them from ſucceeding each other, either riſing or falling; the ſame may be ſaid of two eighths. I believe moſt people think that a uniſon is very eaſily ſtruck; but I would have them keep this truth in mind, viz. if one voice vibrates a thouſand times in a ſecond, and the other nine hundred and ninety nine, they are not in uniſon.

Scholar.

Scholar. Sir, I ſhould be glad to know which you think is to be preferred in a ſinger, a good voice or a good ear.

Maſter. A good ear is as much preferable to a good voice, as good eye ſight is to a good looking glaſs, for the ear is governour of the voice as much as the helm is governour of the ſhip; for when I attempt to ſtrike a certain ſound, my ear informs me whether I am right or wrong, and if wrong, whether I am too high or too low; without which information, I ſhould not be able to ſing one tune, nor ſtrike one note rightly, but by mere chance, for any one that has not a muſical ear* is no better judge of muſical ſounds, than a blind man is of colours, and you may take it for granted, that any one who has a curious ear, with an indifferent voice, will harmonize much better in concert, than one who has an excellent voice with an indifferent ear.

Scholar. Have you ever heard it obſerved what part of this globe is moſt productive of muſical performers.

Maſter. I have often heard it remarked by travellers, that the people who live near the torrid zone, are in general more muſical than thoſe who border upon the frigid. I have made one obſervation which induces me to believe this remark to be juſt, viz. the blacks who are brought here from Africa, are in general better conſtituted for muſic, than the natives of North America; indeed nature ſeems to have laviſhly beſtowed on them, all the mechanical powers requiſite to conſtitue muſical performers, for they have ſtrong lungs, they are remarkably long winded, they have muſical ears, and very melodious voices. N. B. This remark will not apply to blacks born in this country, for their voices are but indifferent.

Scholar. What is an Anthem?

Maſter. It is a divine ‡ ſong, generally in proſe, and although I have often heard it diſputed, yet I think any piece of divine muſic, that is not divided into metre (excepting canons and chanting pieces) may with propriety be called an *Anthem.*

Scholar.

* I think we may with propriety make a diſtinction between thoſe who (are ſaid to) have a muſical ear, and thoſe who have an ear for muſic; for any who are pleaſed and entertained with muſical ſounds, may be ſaid to have an ear for muſic, but before they can *juſtly* be ſaid to have a muſical ear, they muſt be able to make very nice diſtinctions.

‡ I have heard ſome object to this definition, becauſe it was a partial one, for they ſay that all divine words when ſet to muſic, may with propriety be called divine ſongs, whether in proſe or verſe.—In anſwer, I grant that the remark is very pertinent; but as words were made to convey ideas, and different names were given to different things, for the ſake of diſtinguiſhing one thing from another: I have (for the ſake of *convenience*) diſtinguiſhed *Anthems* from *Pſalm-tunes* in the manner above mentioned.

Scholar. Why may not the Italians be deemed uncharitable who ſay, that "*God loves* not *him* who *loves* not *muſic?*"

Maſter. Becauſe they well know that there are no ſuch beings. For as our organs of ſenſe, are differently conſtructed; ſo our notions of ſenſitive things are proportionably various, and this variety gave birth to a proverb which is common among us, viz "What is *one* man's *meat* is *another* man's *poiſon.*" Therefore the *pſalmodiſt* hears *muſic*, in a compoſition of *church muſic*: The *valiant ſoldier*, in the ſound of the *fife* and *drum*, in the *roaring of cannon* and *whiſtling* of *bullets*: The *fearful ſoldier*, in the midnight cry of "*all is well*:" The *huntſman*, in the *ſound* of the *horn* and *cry* of the *hounds*: The *ſtageplayer*, in the *clap* of *applauſe*: The *centinel*, in the *ſound* of "*relief guard*:" The *merchant*, in the *ſound* of *cent* per *cent*: The *uſurer*, in the *ſound* of *intereſt* upon *intereſt*: The *miſer*, in the *ſound* of his *double jo's*, *moidores* and *guineas*. To the two laſt mentioned, we may add another animal by far the nobleſt of the three, viz. the *horſe*, who hears *muſic*, in the *ſound* of his *provender*, *rattling* from the *pottle* to the *trough*. Therefore as muſic is nothing more than agreeable ſounds, certainly that ſound which is moſt pleaſing is moſt muſical. Theſe things conſidered; let us exclude thoſe only who are not bleſt with the faculty of hearing, and then we may (without preſumption) join the Italians and ſay, "*God loves* not *them* who *love* * not *muſic.*"

Scholar. Sir, I thank you, for your kind inſtructions; I think I have no more queſtions to aſk † at preſent, but your advice will always be gratefully received by your much obliged pupil.

Maſter.

* I think the Friends are the only religious ſect, who exclude muſic from their devotions; but, although it is againſt their principles, yet it is not always againſt their conſtitutions: which ſometimes occaſions their getting behind doors, or under windows, to gratify an itching ear—which they happened to be born with. One of this ſect was once ſo catholic as to allow two of her neices to attend my ſchool, and I obſerved that ſhe came almoſt every evening, "to ſee the girls ſafe home," as ſhe expreſſed it; and what is moſt diverting is, that ſhe always came an hour or more before ſchool broke up, and that was, as ſhe ſaid, "to be there in ſeaſon;" but her pretentions were ſo thin, they were eaſily ſeen through, for if I am not much out of my conjectures, ſhe was as highly entertained as any of the audience. And yet this woman would never acknowledge that muſic was any gratification to her, nor would ſhe allow it to be practiſed in her houſe. An arch Wag brought her a fiddle to play on, ſhe reſented it highly; upon which he told her the following ſtory. "Once on a time all the beaſts met together in order for diverſion, they were all for muſic but the *Devil* and the *Aſs*, chuſe which you will."

† *Scholar.* Farewell Preceptor!

Maſter. Farewell! dear pupil, your pertinent interrogations, have ſweetly extorted many remarks and digreſſions from your loving preceptor; and if you are as much edified in the reception, as I was delighted, in the conveyance of theſe broken hints and imperfect ideas, the ſatisfaction on my ſide will fully compenſate for all my trouble; and I take this opportunity to recommend your inquiſitive turn of mind to all my pupils, for the anſwers edify (not only the interrogator, but) all within hearing.

Maſter. I adviſe you to be neither too confident, nor too diffident, that is, do not be too ready to give up your argument, when your cauſe may be juſt and well grounded, and on the other hand, do not be ſwallowed up, in ſelf-will nor ſelf-conceit, but let your mind be always open to conviction, diligently enquiring after truth; for *Solomon* ſays, "*inſtruct a wiſe man and he will yet be wiſer.*" Therefore you muſt never think yourſelf too wiſe * to be taught, nor too old to learn; but be always ready to receive inſtruction from any one; and I hope you will be able to ſay with the *Pſalmiſt*, "*I have more underſtanding than all my teachers.*" At the ſame time you muſt not be ſo taken up with the *ſound* as to neglect the *ſubſtance*, but ſtrive to ſing in the ſpirit as well as with the underſtanding: and *God* grant we may ſo conduct ourſelves here, as to be admitted into that land of *Harmony*, † where we may in tuneful Hoſannahs and eternal Hallelujahs, Shout the REDEEMER.

THE

* There is a very ſtriking paſſage recorded in Eccleſiaſticus, viz. "*he that is not wiſe will not be taught*," a concluſive argument that ignorance and conceit are inſeparable companions. To illuſtrate this more fully, take one inſtance. In my muſical excurſions through the country, I became acquainted with a ſuperannuated old *Deacon*, who had officiated as choriſter in his pariſh upwards of thirty years ſucceſſively. He frequently told me, that he underſtood the ſcale of muſic perfectly: and by cloſe application and ſevere ſtudy, he had found out that there was no half tones in nature, but that their imaginary exiſtence was introduced by pedantic ſinging maſters to keep people in ignorance in order to fleece them of their money. This ſame gentleman happening to be at ſome diſtance from home was invited to attend a monthly lecture: where, without being deſired, he undertook to ſet the pſalm, which happened to be long metre. The Deacon ſtruck St. Martin's, "that wont do." Then New-Glouceſter—"nor that." Then Wantage—"never the nearer."—He then made an effort to ſing Bangor, but was ſagacious enough to diſcover his miſtake, by the time he had ended the *ſecond* line. In this interval or ceſſation of ſound one of the congregation ſet Buckland, which relieved the poor Deacon for that time.—After divine ſervice was ended, one of his acquaintance interrogates the Deacon in the following manner. "How now! Deacon, what a man of your vaſt abilities in muſic make ſuch *intolerable* blunders? To which the Deacon (by way of reſentment) made the following reply. "Do not blame me, blame the miniſter, for it is vaſtly out of character in him to give out a long metre Pſalm, on a Lecture day."

†———"where they introduce
The ſacred ſong; and waken raptures high:
No one exempt, no voice but well could join
Melodious part: ſuch concord is in heaven."—MILTON.

THE CONTINENTAL HARMONY, &c.

:S: *An Anthem, for Thankſgiving.* Pſalm 148.

praiſe him, praiſe him all ye angels, praiſe him all ye angels,
praiſe him all ye angels, praiſe him, praiſe him all ye angels, praiſe, praiſe Je - hovah, praiſe Je - hovah,
praiſe him all ye angels, praiſe him, praiſe him, praiſe,
praiſe him all ye angels, praiſe him, praiſe him all ye angels,
Praiſe the Lord, praiſe the Lord, praiſe the Lord, Let them praiſe the
praiſe him ſun and moon and blaz - ing comets,

name of the Lord,
and they were created, ad–
For he ſpake the word and all were made, he com - manded and they were cre - ated,
mire, adore, admire adore.
Change your dire
Ye dargons* whoſe contageous breath,
People the dark a - bodes of death,

* Roſcommon.

hiffings in - to heav'nly fongs, And praife, your maker with your forked
Fork-
Fork - ed
fork - ed, tongues, with your forked,
forked, tongues, with your forked tongues, and praife your Maker
ed fork - ed
forked forked

with your for - ked tongues, O praiſe the Lord of heaven
fire, hail and ſnow,
wind and ſtorms,
beaſts & cattle, creeping inſects, flying fowl, kings & princes, men & angels praiſe the Lord, Jew & Gentile, male & ſemale, bond & free, earth & heaven,

land & water, praiſe the Lord, young men & maids, old men & babes praiſe the Lord, join creation, preſervation, and redemption join in
one ; no exemption, nor diſſention, one invention, and intention, reigns through the whole, to praiſe the Lord, praiſe the Lord.

Hal - le - lu - jah, hal - le - lujah, hal - le - lujah, hal - le - lu - jah, hal - le lu - jah,
prai - - - - - - fe the Lord.

An Anthem, for Faſt Day. Iſaiah, Chap. 1ſt.

Set this piece in E.

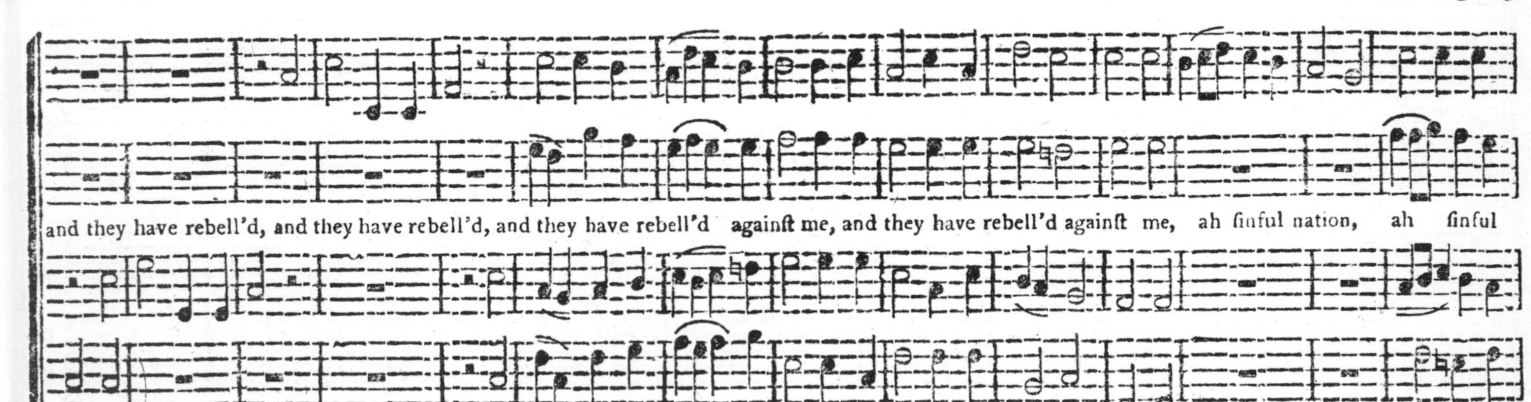

nation. The ox knows his owner, the afs his mafter's crib, but Ifr'el doth not know, but Ifr'el doth not know, but Ifr'el doth not

know, my people doth not confider, Ah finful nation, ah finful nation.

A people laden with iniquity, a feed of evil

pro - voked, provoked,
Children, that are corruptors, they have for - ſak - en the Lord, they have provoked, provoked, pro - vok - ed the holy
pro - vok - ed,
provoked
one of Iſr'el unto anger. Ah ſinful nation, ah ſinful nation, Waſh ye make ye clean, put away the

evil of your doings from before mine eyes, learn to do well, feek judgment, relieve the oppreffed, judge the
ceafe to do evil, judge the
plead, for the widow, plead,
plead, for the widow do
plead, for the widow, plead,
fatherlefs, plead for the widow, plead for the widow, plead, plead,

justice, love mercy, walk humbly before God, Come now let us reason together, reason together, saith the Lord,
though your sins they be as scarlet they shall be as wool, though they be read like crimson, like crimson, like

ſnow
crimſon, yet they ſhall be as white as ſnow, as white as ſnow, yet they ſhall be as white as ſnow.
ſnow
Great-Plain. Words from Dr. Watts.
Ye ſlumb'ring ſaints a heav'nly hoſt, ſtands waiting at your gaping tombs, let ev'ry ſacred ſleeping

☞ Part of this tune is very badly bar'd, but I will leave it for the obſervation of the reader.

Rocky-Nook. :S:

Words from Dr. Watts.

how came they to the

Those glor'ous minds how bright they shine, Whence all their white array, How came they to the happy seats of

How came they to the happy

How came they to the happy, happy :S: seats

hap - py seats of everlasting day.

:S:

everlasting day.. How came, &c.

seats, How came, &c.

How came they to the happy seats, How came, &c.

G

West-Sudbury. Words from Mr. John Peck

Norfolk. Words by Dr. Watts.

Let the old heathen tune their ſong, Of great Di - ana and of Jove, But the ſweet theme that moves my tongue, Is the Re-

:S: :S:

deemer and his love, But the ſweet theme that moves my tongue, Is the Re - deemer and his love.

Creation. Words by Dr. Watts.

Strange that a harp of thoufand
tains a thoufand ftrings, and dies if one be gone.
Strange that a harp of thoufand
Strange that a harp of thoufand ftrings fhould
Strange that a harp of thoufand ftrings, Should keep in tune fo
ftrings, Should keep in tune fo long, fhould keep in tune, fhould keep in tune fo long, fhould keep in tune fo long, fhould
ftrings, Should keep in tune fo long, Strange that a harp of thoufand ftrings, Should keep in tune, fhould keep in tune fo fo
keep in tune fo long, fhould keep in tune fo long, fhould keep in tune fo long, fhould
long, Strange that a harp of thoufand ftrings, Should keep in tune fo long, fhould keep in tune fo long, fhould

keep in tune ſo long, Strange that a harp of thouſand ſtrings, Should keep in tune ſo long, ſo long, ſo
- - - ng, Our life contains a thouſand ſprings and dies if one be gone, Strange that a harp of
keep in tune ſo long, Strange that a harp of thouſand ſtrings, Should keep in tune ſo lo - - - - - -
long, Strange that a harp of thouſand ſtrings, Should keep in tune ſo long
long, ſhould keep in tune ſo long, ſhould keep in tune ſo long, &c.
thouſand ſtrings, Should keep in tune ſo long, ſhould keep in tune ſo long, ſo long, Strange that a harp of thouſand ſtrings, Should keep in tune ſo long.
- - ng, ſhould keep in tune ſo long,
Strange that a harp of thouſand ſtrings, Should keep in tune, ſhould keep in tune ſo long,

St. John's.

Words by Dr. Watts.

Where are the mourners, &c.

Croſs-Street.
Words from Addiſon.
The Lord my paſture ſhall prepare, And feed me with a ſhepherd's care, His preſence ſhall my wants ſupply, And guard me with a watchful eye.
:S:
:S:
My noonday walk he ſhall attend, And all my midnight hours defend, And all my, &c.

Majeſtic God our muſe inſpire, And fill us with ſe - raphic fire, Augment our ſwells, our

:S:

Aug-

tones re - fine, Per - formance ours, the glory thine. Augment our ſwells, our tones refine, Per-

Augment our ſwells, our

ment our ſwells our tones refine, performance ours the glory thine, &c.
formance ours the glory thine, the glory thine, the glory thine, Per - formance ours the glory thine.
tones refine, Performance ours, &c.
Bellingham. Words by Dr. Watts.
Begin my tongue ſome heav'nly theme, And ſpeak ſome boundleſs thing, The mighty works or mighty name, Of

our eternal King, Tell of his wond'rous faithfulnefs, And found his pow'r abroad, Sing the fweet promife of his grace, And the performing God, And the performing God.
Cobaffet. Words by Dr. Watts.
Life is the time to ferve the Lord, The time t'in - fure the great re-

ward, And while the lamp holds out to burn, The vil - eſt ſinner may return.
:S:
:S:
And while the lamp, &c.
And while the lamp holds out to burn, The vileſt ſinner may return.
And while the lamp, &c.
And while the lamp, &c.

Egypt. Words by Dr. Watts. :S:
Come fee the wonders, fee the wonders, fee the wonders of our God, How glor'ous are his ways,
In Mofes hand he
In Mofes hand he
In Mofes hand he puts his rod, And
In Mofes hand he puts his rod, And cleaves the frighted feas, And cleaves the frighted feas, and cleaves the frighted
puts his rod, And cleaves the frighted feas, and cleaves the frighted feas, and cleaves the frighted feas, and
puts his rod and cleaves the frighted feas, and cleaves the frighted :||: feas,
cleaves the frighted feas, and cleaves the frighted feas, and cleaves and

feas, cleaves, and cleaves, and cleaves, and cleaves, &c.

cleaves the frighted feas, and cleaves, and cleaves the frighted feas, and cleaves the frighted feas, and cleaves the frighted feas.

come fee the wonders of our God, How glor'ous are his ways, In Mofes hand he puts his rod, And cleaves, &c.

cleaves, and cleaves the frighted feas, and cleaves, and cleaves, and cleaves the, &c.

Revelation. Words by Dr. Watts.

Let all the heathen writers join, To form one perfect book; Great God if once compar'd with thine, How mean their writings

:S:

How mean their writings look, Great God if

look. Great God if once compar'd with thine, Great God if once compar'd with

How mean, how mean their writings look, how

How mean their writings look, how mean, how mean their writings

once, Great God if once compar'd with thine, &c.

thine, how mean, how mean, their writings look, how mean, how mean their writings look

mean, how mean their writings look, how mean, &c.

look, how mean their writings look, &c.

Washington-Street. Words by Dr. Watts.

mighty love inſpires my heart, And pleaſure tunes, and pleaſure tunes my tongue, Al - mighty love in-
pleaſure tunes, and pleaſure tunes, and pleaſure tunes, and pleaſure tunes my tongue,
mighty love inſpires my heart, And pleaſure tunes my tongue.
:S:
ſpires my heart, And pleaſure tunes, and pleaſure tunes my tongue.
I

Thomas-Town. Words by Dr. Biles.

St. Enoch. *For a Thanksgiving, after a Victory.*

Sing, Sing to the Lord a new made ſong, Who wond'rous things has done, who wond'rous things has done, who wond'rous wond'rous things has done,

Sing, Sing to the Lord a new made ſong, Who wond'rous, who wond'rous things has done, who wond'rous, wond'rous things has done.

Sing, ſing, ſing who wond'rous, who wond'rous, who wond'rous things has done,

Sing, Sing, to the Lord a new made ſong, Who wond'rous, who wond'rous things has done, who wond'rous things has done.

:S: :S:

with his right hand and holy arm, the conqueſt he has won the conqueſt he has won.

with his right hand and holy arm the conqueſt he has won, &c.

with his right hand and ho - ly arm the conqueſt, the conqueſt, the conqueſt the conqueſt, &c.

With his right hand and holy arm the conqueſt, the conqueſt, the conqueſt, the conqueſt he has won, &c.

Morning Hymn. :S: Words by Dr. Watts.

West-Sudbury. Words by Mr. John Peck.

What if the faint muſt die, And lodge among the tombs; He need not mourn he ſhall return, Rejoicing as he comes. Though

:S:

death ſhould hold him down, With bands and mighty bars; Yet he ſhall riſe above the ſkies, And ſing above the ſkies.

:S: *An Anthem. For Thanksgiving Day Morning.*

:S:

life forevermore, is life for - ever, is life for - ev - er more. Sing

and in his favour is life forevermore. Sing praifes,

life, is life, is life for - ev - ermore. Sing praifes,

life, is life for - ev - ermore, is life Sing praifes,

:S: :S:

1 2

praif es, fing praifes, fing praifes, fing praifes to the Lord O ye faints of his, for his wrath endures but a moment and in his

and in his favour, in his favour is life, is life forevermore, and in his favour, his favour is
favour, in his favour is life forevermore A - men, is life forevermore, is life forevermore,
for - e - vermore, is life, is life, is li-
life, is life, is life, is life is
:S·
life, is life for - ev - er - more. For his wrath endures but a moment, is life is
and in his favour is life forevermore. and in his favour is life, is life, is
- fe, is life, for - ev - ermore.
life for - ev - er - more

life, is life, is life forevermore, is life forever - more, and in his favour, in his favour is

life, is life, is life, is life forevermore and in his favour, his favour is life, in his favour is

for - ever - more, is life, is li - -

life, is life for - ev - er -

:S:

life, is life, is life forevermore. Heavineſs may endure for a night but joy but

life is life forevermore, forevermore. may indure for a night but

- fe, &c. may endure for a night but joy but

more, is life, &c. Heavineſs may endure for a night,

K

:S:
joy cometh in the morning, &c.
joy, but joy cometh in the morning, but joy cometh in the morning, but joy, but joy, but joy, but joy cometh in the morning.
joy, but joy, but joy, but joy, &c.
Weymouth. Words by Dr. Watts.
Shall we go on to fin, Becaufe thy grace abounds. Or cru-ci-fy the Lord again, And open all his

:S:
Or cru - ci - fy the Lord again, And open all his
wounds. Cr cruci - fy the Lord again, And open all his
Or cru - ci - fy the Lord a - gain, And open all his
Or cru - ci - fy the Lord again, Or cru - ci - fy the Lord again, And open all his
:S:
wounds. Or crucify the Lord again and open all his wounds, and open all his wounds.
wounds. Or cru - ci - fy the Lord a - gain, and open all his wounds.
o - - - - - - - pen all his wounds.
cru - ci - fy the Lord a - gain and open all, &c.

An Anthem. Solomon's Songs, Chap. 5th.

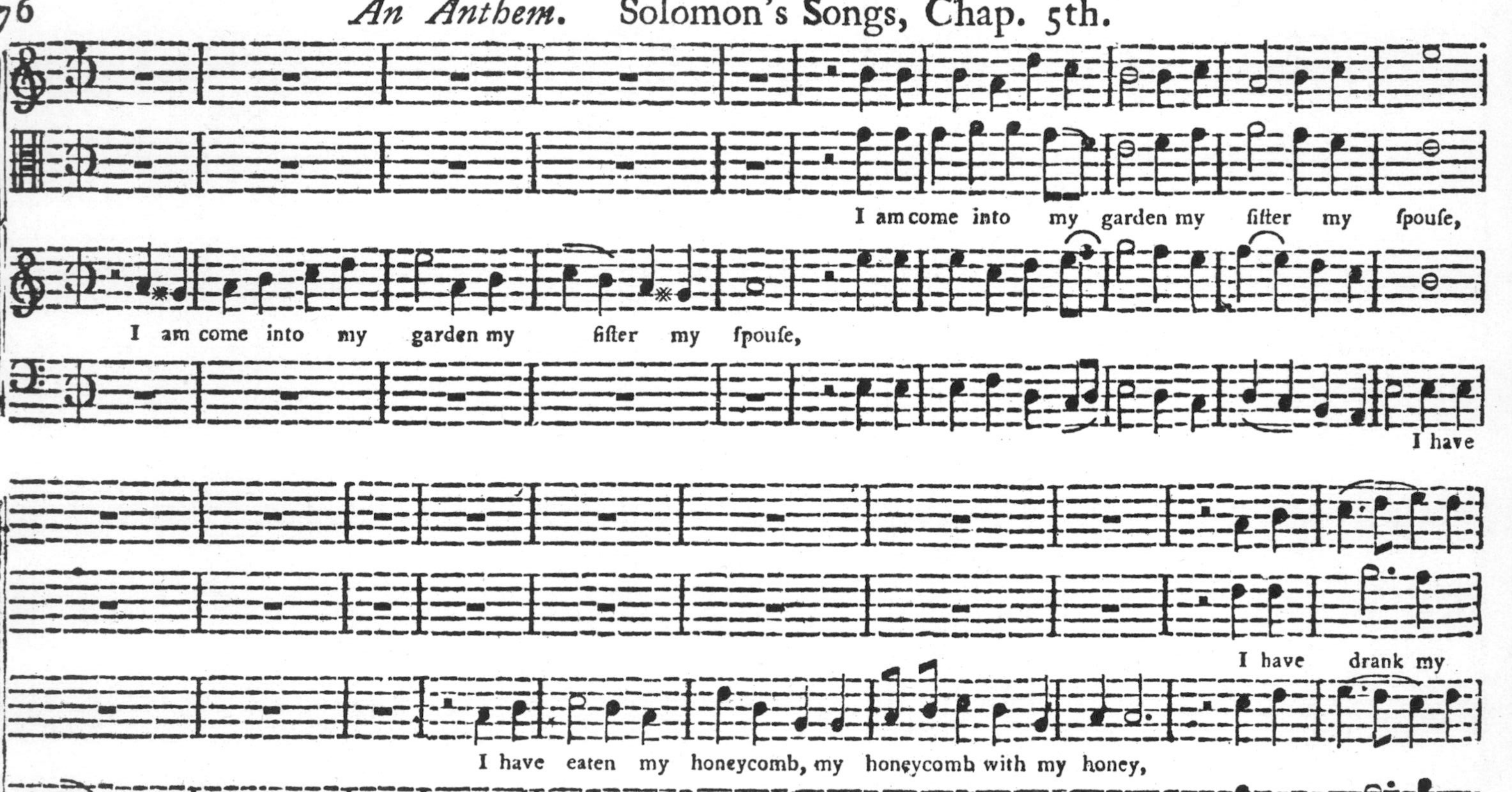

:S:
eat O friends a - bundantly, and drink O friends a - bundantly, and
wine with my milk, eat, eat, O friends, drink, drink O friends, eat, eat, eat, eat O friends a-
eat, eat, eat, eat, eat,
eat O friends a - bundantly, a - bundantly, abundantly, and
dnk O friends a - bundant - ly, eat O friends, and drink O friends, eat,
undantly, eat O friends abundant - ly, eat O friends abundantly, drink O friends abundant - ly,
eat abundantly, a - bundantly, a - bundantly, and eat a - bundantly, a - bundantly, and
ank O friends a - bundantly, eat, eat O friends, eat, eat, drink, drink O friends,

:S:
eat O friends a - bundantly,
I ſleep, but my heart waketh, it is the voice of my be loved ſayig,
open to me
for my head is fill'd with dew and ıy
my ſiſter, my love, my dove, my un - de - filed,

I open'd to my be - loved, but my be - loved had withdrawn himself,
locks with the drops of the night.
and he was gone, I fought him, I fought him but I could not find him, I call'd him, I call'd him, I
and he was gone,

Stay me with flagons, comfort me with apples for I am
call'd him, I call'd him but he gave me no anſwer.
:S: Vigoroſo.
ſick of love.
Make haſte my beloved, make haſte my beloved, and be like a roe, and be like a roe.

be like a roe or a young hart upon the mountains, the mountains, the mountains, the mountains the mountains the mountains of ſpices.
Rocheſter.
:S:
Words by the Rev. George Whitefield.
Ye ſervants of God, your Maſter proclaim, And publiſh abroad, his wonderful name; The name all victor'ous, of Jeſus extol, His kingdom is glor'ous, and rules over all.

Gilead. :S:

Words by Dr. Watts.

South-Boston. Words by Dr. Watts.

Join all the glorious names, Of wisdom love and pow'r, That ever mortals knew, That angels ever bore. All are too mean to speak his worth, Too mean to set my Sa - viour forth.

An Anthem. Pſalm 44th.

Suitable to be ſung on the anniverſary of our Fore-fathers' landing, and for Thankſgiving.

ſword nor by their bow,
But thy right hand and holy arm, and the light of thy countenance,
becauſe thou hadſt a favour unto them, be thou our king O God, command de - liv - erance, com-
3/2
3/2
3/2
3/2

b key.
mand de - liverance for Jacob, be thou our king, O God command deliverance for Jacob, Awake, why
ſleepeſt thou O Lord ariſe ariſe caſt us not off forever caſt us not off forever.
for ſo the wicked have

To ſhoot, to ſhoot, to ſhoot at the righteous privily, to ſhoot at the righteous privily,
bent their bow
:S:
O Lord we acknowledge we have ſinned, O Lord we acknowledge we have ſinned, O
O Lord we acknowledge we have ſinned, we acknowledge we have ſinned, we acknowledge we have ſinned,
O Lord we acknowledge, we have ſinned, we acknowledge, we have ſinned, we acknowledge we have ſinned, before
O Lord we acknowledge we have ſinned, we acknowledge we have ſinned, we acknowledge we have ſinned,

Lord we acknowledge we have finned before thee and are not worthy, are not worthy, we are &c.
we acknowledge we have finned, we are not worthy, we are not worthy, we are not worthy, not worthy to be called thy children
thee and are not worthy, are not worthy, are not worthy to be called thy children, we are not worthy &c.
we acknowledge we have finned, we are not worthy we are not worthy, we are, &c.

hear us, hear us, hear us, hear us from heav'n, and when thou hear'ft forgive and when thou hear'ft forgive.

Father of mercy, God of conso - lation hear us, hear from heav'n thy dwelling place, and when thou hear'ſt for-
- give, and when thou hear'ſt, forgive. Ariſe, :||: O Lord, gird on thy ſword, moſt mighty prince, put on thy ſtrength moſt

Vigoroſo.
mighty Lord, Ride upon the heavens for our help, and in thy majeſty upon the ſkies ride upon the heavens
for our help, and in thy majeſty upon the ſkies, then the heathen will acknowledge that the Lord he is God then the heathen will ac-

knowledge that the Lord he is God.
The enemy said I will bran dish my ſword, I will flour ish my
thou didſt blow,
ſword, my hand ſhall demoliſh then my hand ſhall devour then
thou didſt blow,

Fortiſſimo.
thou didſt blow with thy wind
the Lord ſhall reign for ever and
they ſunk like lead in the mighty :𝄆: waters,
:S:
ever ſhall reign for ever, for - ever and ever,
for this cauſe I will give
for this cauſe I will give thanks, and
for this cauſe I will give thanks, for this cauſe I will give

for this cause I will give thanks, and praise his holy name, praise ye the
thanks and praise his holy name, and praise his holy name, praise ye the
praise his holy name, and praise his &c. praise thou the
thanks, and praise his holy name, and praise his &c. praise ye the
Lord the Lord's name be praised, praised, the Lord, the Lord's name be praised, and let all the people say ame-
Lord O my soul, praise ye the Lord Hall - le - lu - jah, for this cause I will give thanks
Lord, the Lord's name be praised praise ye the Lord the Lord's name be praised Hallelu - jah, halle - lu - jah,
Lord and all that is within me, praise ye the Lord, the Lord's name be praised, for this cause I will give thanks,

- - - en, &c. A - men, a - m-
and praife his holy name, and let all the people fay a - men, a - men, and let all the people fay amen,
a - men, amen, &c. and let all the people fay, and let
and praife his holy name, &c. :S: a - men, amen,
en, a - men, &c.
a - men, - a - men amen, praife ye the Lord a - men, amen.
all the people fay a - men, &c.
a - men, :||: :||: :||:

Dedham.

Words by Dr. Watts.

Rejoice ye ſhining worlds on high. Behold the king of glory nigh. Who

:S:

can this king of glo - ry be, The mighty Lord and Sa - viour's he Who

Who can this king of glo - ry be, The mighty, mighty
Who can this king, this king of glory be, The
Who can this king of glo - ry be, The mighty mighty
can this king of glo - ry be, The mighty mighty, Lord and :S: Sa - viour's
Lord, the mighty, mighty, mighty Lord and Saviour's he, &c.
mighty, mighty Lord, the mighty, :||: :||: :||: Lord and Saviour's he.
mighty Lord and Saviour's he, The mighty :||: :||: Lord and, &c.
be, the mighty, mighty, mighty Lord and Sa - viour's he, &c.

Univerſal Praiſe : An Anthem, for *Thankſgiving Day*, taken from Pſalm 149, &c.

O praiſe God, O praiſe God, O praiſe God, praiſe him in his holineſs, praiſe him propagation, praiſe him vegetation, and let your voice, pro-

claim your choice, & teſtiſy, to ſtanders by, with ardent fire, your firm deſire, to praiſe, praiſe, praiſe, praiſe, praiſe the Lord.

Let the leading baſs in-

N

Anthem. Continued.

Let the treble join the choir,

Let the counter ſtill be high'r, until all the parts have join'd the choir, Let all agree and join with me, to praiſe, praiſe,

Let the tenor catch the fire, and ſpecify their firm deſire, until all the parts have join'd the choir,

ſpire, and ſtimulate with ardent fire, Ardent, ardent fire, until all the parts have join'd the choir,

praiſe, praiſe, praiſe the Lord. Shout ye hills and ſing ye plains, tell the earth Jehovah reigns, ſound the trumpets, beat the drums, tell the

roll the drums, roll the drums, found the trumpets, roll the drums,
earth Jehovah comes. Sound the trumpets, roll the drums, found the trumpets, beat the drums, beat, beat, beat, the drum,
trum - pets , found the trumpets, trum - pets, roll the drums,
roll the drums, found the trumpets, beat the drums, beat, beat, beat the drums.
found the trumpets, beat the drums, found the trumpets ro - - - - - - ll the drums, tell the earth

Anthem. Continued.

ſign, young men and maids, old men and babes, u - nanimouſly join, let all agree, and join with me, to praiſe, praiſe,
praiſe, praiſe praiſe the Lord, Let the organ ſtrike a chord, and ſound the praiſe of Jubal's God, let the organ ſtrike a

Anthem. Continued.

bleat, and ſound, ſound, ſound, ſound and ſound their maker's praiſe, their voice for ſhame and catch the flame of u - ni - ver - ſal
praiſe, praiſe, praiſe, praiſe, praiſe the Lord, Let the hearers fill their part, tho' mute in voice yet join in heart and praiſe

:S: *Anthem*. Continued.

Hal-le - lujah, halle - lu - jah, halle-

praise, praise, praise, praise the Lord, A - men, a - men, a - men, Halle - lujah praise, praise the

Amen, Hal - le - lujah

Halle - lu - jah, halle - lujah, halle lujah, halle-

:S:

lujah a - men, a - men, praise, praise the Lord, a - men,

Lord a - men, a - men, Halle - lujah, A - men, a - men, a - men, a–men, Halle - lujah, halle - lujah a - men,

- men, a - men, a-men,

lujah a - men.

An Anthem for Ordination. Words from Tate & Brady, Scripture, &c.

O thou to whom all creatures bow, Within this earthly frame, Thro' all the world how

:S:

great art thou, How glorious is thy name. Thro' all the

Thro'

Thro' all the world how

O

Thro' all the world how great art thou, in all, &c.
world how great art thou, in all, in all, in all this earth - ly frame.
all the world how great art thou in all, in all, &c.
great art thou, in all, in all, in all, in all, &c.
That they may
And he ſhall purify the ſons of Levi, and purge them as gold aud ſilver,

I will deck her priests with
offer un - to the Lord an off'ring, an off'ring in righteousness.
health.
shout shall shout
I will deck her priests with health and her saints shall shout shall
health,
shout, shall shou - - -

- ut, ſhall ſhout, ſhall ſho - - ut and her ſaints &c.

ſhout, ſhall ſhout and ſing, ſhall ſhout and ſing, ſhall &c.

ſhout, ſhall ſhout, ſhall ſhout, ſhall ſhout and

- ut, ſhall ſhout, ſhall ſhout, and ſing and her ſaints ſhall

Pia. Forte.

ſing, Hal - le - lujah, hal - le-lu-jah, hal - le - lujah, I will deck her prieſts with health,

and her ſaints ſhall ſhout, and her ſaints ſhall ſhout, and her &c.
I will deck her prieſts with health, and her ſaints ſhall ſhout, and her ſaints ſhall ſhout, and her ſaints ſhill ſhout, ſhall
and her ſaints ſhall ſhout, and her ſaints ſhall ſhout and ſing,
ſhout and ſing, ſhall ſhout and ſing, and her ſaints ſhall ſho - -
and her ſaints ſhall ſhout.

- - - ut, ſhall ſhout and ſing, then the eyes of the blind, ſhall be open'd.
and the ears of the
Glory be to thee O Lord, glory be to thee O Lord,
deaf ſhall be unſtopped
for how can they hear with-

the Lord gave the word, the

and how shall they preach except they be sent, the Lord gave the word, the Lord gave the

the Lord gave the word, the Lord gave the word the

out a preacher, the Lord gave the word,

Lord gave he word, and

worrd, and great was the company of preachers, the Lord gave the word, the Lord gave the word, the Lord gave the word, and

Lord gave the word, and

great was the company of preachers, How beautiful, how beautiful, how beautiful, up-
on the mountaints, are the feet of him that bringeth good tidings, that publisheth peace, peace,

:S:
peace, peace be on earth good will towards men.
Sym. to introduce B flat.
The great high
The great high prieſt, the
The great high prieſt the glo'rous work the
The great high prieſt the glo'rous work has done, and ſhouting, &c.
prieſt, the glo'rous work has done, and ſhouting ſeraphs, ſhouting ſeraphs, ſeraphs bear him to his throne.
glo'rous work has done, and ſhouting ſeraphs, ſhouting ſeraphs, ſhouting ſeraphs bear him to his throne.
glo'rous work has done and ſhou - ting ſeraphs bear him to his throne. Then
P

Then while the heav'ns re - found with ju - be-
Then while the heav'ns re - found, refound with Ju - bi-
Then while the heav'ns re - found with Ju - bi - lee, let mortals raife, let
while the heav'ns re - found with Ju - bi - lee, let mortals raife the gen'ral voice, let
lee let mortals raife the gen'ral voice of joy, of joy, of jcy let, &c.
lee, let mortals raife the gen'ral voice of joy, of jov, of joy, let
mortals raife the gen'ral voice of joy, of joy, of joy, of joy. let
mortals raife the gen'ral, &c.

:S:

mortals raiſe the gen'ral voice of joy, of joy.

:S:

Not unto us O Lord, not unto us but un - to thy name be the glory. Glory be to God on

Glory, glory, peace be on earth Halle - lujah, Good will to men peace be on earth Halle - lujah,

high, Halle - lujah, good will to men, glory, glory, peace be on earth, Halle - lujah, glory, glory,

peace be on earth, glory, glory, good will to men. Halle - lujah, glory, glory, peace be on earth,

Good will to men, Halle - lujah, peace be on earth, glory, glory, good will to men Halle - lujah,

:S:

glory, &c.

:S:

glory to God, peace, good will to men glory to God.

An Anthem for Christmas. Words from Luke 2d. and elsewhere.

N. B. Set this piece one note lower.

:S:
be - hold I bring you glad
thousand, a thousand, a thousand heav'nly echos echos echos cry, be - hold I bring you glad
Behold I bring you glad tidings glad
Behold I bring you glad
tidings, glad tidings, I bring you glad tidings of joy, &c.
tidings, I bring you glad tidings, glad tidings of joy, unto you, unto you and to all people,
For

For unto you this day is born a Saviour, a Saviour which is, &c. and this ſhall be a
For unto you this day is born a Saviour which is, &c.
For unto you this day is born a Saviour a Saviour who is Chriſt the Lord.
unto you this day is born a Saviour, a &c,
:S:
ſign unto you, you ſhall find the babe meanly wrap'd in ſwadling bands and lying in a manger. And

And ſuddenly there was with the angels a multitude and ſuddenly there
And ſuddenly there was with the angels a multitude, a multitude
And ſuddenly there was with the angels a multitude, a multitude, a multitude of the heavn'ly
ſuddenly there was with the angels a multitude a multitude of the heav'nly hoſts, the heavn'ly ho-
was with the angels, &c.
of the heav'nly hoſts, a multitude a multitude of the heav'nly hoſts, and they were praiſing God, and they were praiſing
ſts.

prais - - - - ing, &c.
praising, praising, prais - ing, &c.
. God, and they were prais - ing, prais - ing, prais - - ing, praising God, and saying glory to
God, prais - ing prais ing, &c.
God, glory to God, glory to God in the highest, glory to God in the highest, O how can
Q

men forbear to fing when earth with angels notes do ring, ring, ring, when earth with angels notes do ring, Then
join all your voices one chorus to raife afcribing all honour all glory and praife, What greater love what greater

:S:
:S: :S:
gift, can God, on man beſtow, 'Tis half the angel's heav'n above, And all our heav'n below. Then join all your voices, one
S:
chorus to raiſe, aſcribing all honour all glory and praiſe. Lord, and ſhall angels have their ſongs, and

men no tunes to raiſe, O may we loſe theſe uſeleſs tongues when they forget to praiſe, praiſe, praiſe, When they forget to
praiſe, Then join, &c. Glory to God who reigns a - bove, that pitied us for - lorn we join to ſing our
See Chorus.

maker's love for there's a Saviour born. Halle - lujah, Halle - lujah, Halle - lujah, Hoſannah, in the
highеſt, Halle - lujah, Hoſannah in the higheſt, Hoſannah in the higheſt. What greater love, what greater

gift can God on man be - flow, 'Tis half the an - gels heav'n a-

bove and a - - - - - ll our heav'n below, and all, and all our heav'n be-

- low 'tis half the Angels heav'n a - bove and all, all, all our heav'n below.
1
2
St. Thomas. Words from Dr. Watts.
Methinks I ſee my Saviour dear, On the accurſed tree, Methinks I ſee his bleeding wounds, which he receiv'd for me.

:S:
:S:
Infinite grief a-maz-ing woe behold, our bleeding Lord, Hell and the Jews conſpir'd his death, and us'd the Roman ſword.
'Twere you my ſins my cruel ſins, His chief tormenters were, Each of my crimes became a nail, And unbe lief the

ſpear, 'Twere you that pull'd the vengeance down, Upon his guiltleſs head, Break, break my heart, Oh burſt mine eyes and let my ſorrow bleed.
☞ Obſerve that this tune will contain four verſes.
Broad Cove. :S: Words from Dr. Watts.
Swift as an Indian arrow flies, or
Time, what an empty vapor 'tis, And days how ſwift they are.
Swift as an Indian arrow flies or like a ſhooting
Swift as an Indian arrow flies or like a ſhooting, ſhooting
R
Swift as an Indian arrow flies or like a ſhooting

like a ſhooting, ſhooting, ſhooting, like a ſhooting, ſhoot - ing, ſhooting, ſhooting,
ſhooting, ſhooting, ſhooting like a ſhooting, ſhooting, ſtar or like a ſhooting ſtar or
ſtar, Swift as an Indian arrow flies or like a ſhooting, ſhooting, ſhooting
- - - r, Swift as an Indian ar - row flies or like a ſhooting ſtar, Swift as an Indian
:S:
ſhooting like a ſhooting, ſhoot - ing ſtar,
:S:
like a ſhooting, ſhooting, ſhooting, like a ſhooting ſtar, Swift as an Indian arrow flies or like a ſhooting ſtar.
ſtar, or like a ſhooting, ſhooting ſtar,
rrow flies or like a ſhooting ſtar.

Deliverance, An Anthem. Words from fundry fcriptures, &c.
I will love thee, I will love thee O Lord my ftrength.
In my diftrefs I called to the Lord, and cry'd unto my God and he
Chorus. Soft.
Therefore I will
heard my voice out of his temple, and my cry reached the ear of my God.

Then the earth did sha ke and tremble.
love thee, will love thee, will love thee, therefore I will love thee O Lord my strength.
he bow'd the heav'n's al - so and came down, and darkness was
of the hills were removed and sha - - ken, because he was wroth,

fly, and did fl - y,
and he rode upon a cherub and did fl - - - - - y, yea
fl - y,
under his feet, and darknefs was under his feet, fly, and did fl - - y,
See Chorus.
he did fl - y up - on the wings of the wind, Therefore, &c.
fly did fly
the Lord alfo thunder'd out of heav'n and the higheft gave his

:S:
The Lord alſo thunder'd out of heav'n and the higheſt gave his thunder hail ſtones and coals of fire, and the higheſt gave his
See Chorus.
He deliver'd me from my enemies, and from them which hate me, for
thunder hail ſtones and coals of fire. Therefore, &c.
for
For they were too ſtrong, for

hey were too ſtrong for me, Then I wounded them, Then I wounded them that they were not able to riſe, then they cry'd, then they cry'd, then they
Then I wounded them,
cry'd, then they cry'd, but there was none to hear them. they cry'd unto the Lord, they cry'd unto the Lord but he gave them no anſwer. Then I

trampl'd them down, then I trampl'd them down, then I trampl'd them under my feet. What ſhall I render to my God for all his kindneſs
:S:
Hal - le - lu - jah, hal - le
ſhown my feet ſhall viſit his abode my ſongs addreſs his throne. A - men,
Hal - le - lu - jah, hal - le -
A men,

Swell.

- lujah, Hal - le - lujah, praise the Lord, Amen, amen,

a - men, amen, a - men, Halle - lujah, Halle - lujah, praise the Lord, Hallelujah,

- lujah, halle - lujah, praise the Lord, a - men, amen,

a - men, amen, a - men, hal-le-lu-jah, hal-le-lu-jah, :S:

Forte.

praise, praise the Lord, praise, praise the Lord.

hallelujah, hallelujah, praise, praise, praise, praise, praise the Lord, praise, praise the Lord.

praise the Lord, praise, praise, praise, praise the Lord,

Hallelujah praise, praise, praise, praise, praise

S

O God thou haſt been diſpleaſed, O God thou haſt been diſpleaſed, O God thou haſt been diſ-pleaſ-ed, O turn thee, O turn thee, O
O God thou haſt been diſpleaſed, O God
turn thee unto us again, O turn thee unto us again, thou haſt mov'd the land, and diſturbed it, thou haſt mov'd the

heal the fores, heal the fores, heal the fores there - of,
land and difturbed it, heal the fores, heal the fores, heal the fores thereof, for it fhak - eth, for it
heal the fores, heal the fores, heal the fores there - of,
:S:
fhak - eth, thou haft giv'n a token for fuch as fear thee, that they may tri - umph becaufe of thy truth, may

triumph, may triumph, may triumph because of thy truth, therefore were thy be - lov-ed de-liv-er-ed, hear us hear us
hear us, hear us, hear us, O help us, O help us, O help us with thy right hand and hear us, hear us, help us with thy right hand, and hear us,

Crotchet beating.
Who will lead me, who will lead me into the ſtrong city, who will bring me into Edom, wilt not thou O God go forth with our hoſts, wilt not thou O
God go forth with our hoſts, O help us, O help us, O help us in the time of trouble, for vain, for vain, for vain is the

help of man, through God we ſhall do valiantly, we ſhall do valiantly, we ſhall do valiantly for it is he that ſhall
tread down, tread down our enemies, through God we ſhall do valiantly, we ſhall do valiantly, we ſhall do valiantly for it is he that ſhall

tread down, tread down our enemies. Halleiujah, hallelujah, hallelujah praiſe ye the Lord hal - le - lujah hal - le-
Swell.
lu - jah, halle - lujah, O praiſe, O praiſe, O praiſe the Lord, praiſe, praiſe, the Lord.

Hopkinton.
Words from George Whitefield.
Lo he cometh countless trumpets blow before the bloody sign, midst ten thousand saints and angels see the cru - ci - fi - ed
:S:
:S:
Halle - lujah, halle - lujah, halle - lujah, Welcome, Welcome bleeding Lamb.
shine. Halle - lujah, halle - lujah, halle - lujah Welcome bleeding Lamb, welcome bleeding Lamb.
Welcome, Welcome bleeding Lamb, Welcome
Halle - lujah, halle - lujah, halle - lujah, welcome, welcome bleeding Lamb,

An Anthem, for Fast Day. Some of the words from scripture.

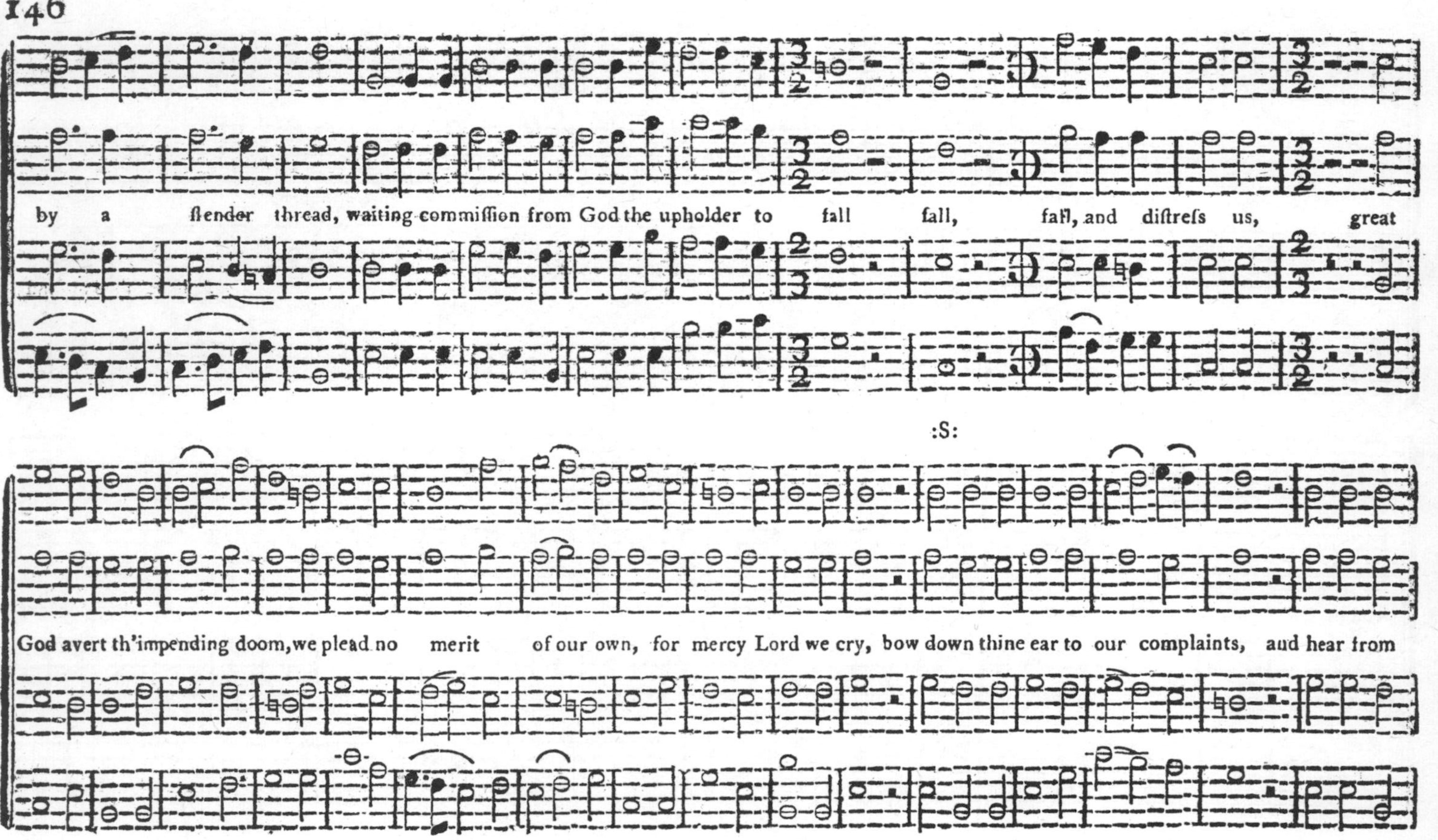
by a ſlender thread, waiting commiſſion from God the upholder to fall fall, fall, and diſtreſs us, great
:S:
God avert th'impending doom, we plead no merit of our own, for mercy Lord we cry, bow down thine ear to our complaints, and hear from

Then will the Lord be jealous for his land and
heav'n thou king of faints, O let thine aid be nigh.
Then will the Lord be jealous for his
Then will the Lord be jealous for his land, and pity his
Then will the Lord be jealous for his land, and
pity his people, and fay behold, behold
no more, no more, no more,
land, and pity his people, and fay behold your Phar'ohs and Achans and Ahabs are no more, no more no more
people, and fay behold be - hold, behold
more, no more, no more,
pity his people, and fay, behold behold,
no more no more,
Yea the

behold, behold I will ſend you corn, and wine, and oil, and ye ſhall be ſatisfy'd,
Lord will anſwer and ſay unto his people,
And
And ye ſhall be ſatisfy'd,
be ſatisfy'd, be ſatisfy'd, be ſatisfy'd therewith, be
And ye ſhall be ſatisfy'd,

Be glad then America,

ſatisfy'd, be ſatisfy'd, be ſatisfy'd therewith. ſhout, ſhout, ſho-

Be glad then Amer - i - ca,

Be glad then America, be glad then America, ſhout, ſhout, and rejoice,

ca, ſhout, :||: ſhout, ſhout and rejoice, ſhout, ſhout, ſhout, ſhout,

ut, be glad then America, ſhout and rejoice, ſhout, ſhout, ſhout, ſhout, ſhout, ſhout, ſhout,

ſhout, ſhout, and rejoice, ſhout, ſhout and rejoice, ſhout, ſhout, ſho-

joice, be glad then America, ſhout, and rejoice, ſhout, ſhout, ſhout and rejoice, ſhout, ſhout and re-

ſhout, ſhout, ſhout, ſhout, ſhout, ſhout, ſhout and rejoice, Fear not O
ſhout and rejoice, ſhout, and rejoice, rejoice, ſhout, and rejoice, Fear not O land, be
ut, ſhout, ſhout, ſhout, ſhout, ſhout, ſhout, and rejoice.
joice, ſhout, ſhout, ſhout, ſhout, ſhout and rejoice, ſhout, Fear not O land be
land be glad be glad and re - - joice, rejoice, fear not O land be glad, be glad, be glad, be
glad and re - joice, rejoice, rejoice, fear not O land be glad, be
fear not O land be glad and re - joice, fear not, &c.
glad and re joice fear not O land, fear not, &c.

:S:
:S: Soft.
Loud.
glad and rejoice, re - joice. Hal - le - lu - jah, hal - le - lu - jah, hal - le - lu - jah.
Soft.
Loud.
:S:
praise the Lord, Hal - le - lu jah, hal - le - lu - jah, hal - le - lu - jah, praise the Lord.

East Sudbury. Words from Dr. Watts.

Adams. Words by Dr. Watts.

Clarimont. A Hymn for Eaſter.

Words Anon.

An Anthem. Solomon's Songs.

If you ſee my be - loved tell him I am ſick of love.
charge you O ye daughters of Jeruſalem,
If you ſee my be-
I charge you, I charge you, I charge you, I charge you that you ſtir not
loved tell her I am ſick of love,

up nor a - wake my love till he pleafe,
What is thy be - loved more than a - nother O thou faireſt
My be - lov - ed is white and ruddy the chief among ten thoufand I
among women,

charge you, I charge you, I charge you, I charge you, that you ſtir not up nor awake my love till he pleaſe.

My be - lov - ed is white and rudy, the

What is thy beloved more than another, O thou faireſt among women,

chief among ten thousand and altogether lovely, his head is as gold, and his eyes are like doves, and his hair is as black as a
raven. I charge you, I charge you, I charge you, I charge you that you stir not up nor awake my love till he please.

An Anthem. Pſalm 126.

:S:

then was our mouths fill'd with laughter, with laughter and joy, then was our mouths fill'd with

gain the captivity of Zion, &c.

:S:

laughter, with laughter, with laughter, with laughter, and joy, for they said among the heathen the Lord hath done great things for

W

:S:
them whereof they are glad, the Lord hath done great things for them whereof they are
the Lord hath done great things for them whereof they are glad, the Lord hath done great
the Lord hath done great things for them where - - of they are
the Lord hath done great things for them whereof they are
glad, &c.
2 1
things for them whereof they are glad, the Lord hath done great things for them whereof they are glad. Turn again our captivity O Lord as the
1 2
glad, the Lord he hath done great things for them whereof they are glad,
1 2
1 2

:S:
for they that ſow in tears ſhall reap in joy, ſhall reap, ſhall reap ſhall
rivers in the ſouth. For they that ſow in tears ſhall reap, in joy, for they that ſow in tears ſhall reap, ſhall
ſhall re - - - - -
for they that ſow in tears ſhall reap in
reap, ſhall reap in joy, ſhall reap in joy, ſhall reap in joy, ſhall reap in joy, for they that ſow in
reap, in joy, ſhall reap, ſhall reap, ſhall reap, in joy, in joy, ſhall reap ſhall
ap in joy, ſhall re - - ap in joy, ſhall reap, ſhall
joy, in joy, for they that ſow in tears ſhall reap in joy, ſhall reap in joy, in

tears, ſhall reap in joy, ſhall reap, ſhall reap, ſhall reap, &c.
reap, ſhall reap in joy, for they that ſow in tears ſhall reap in joy.
reap, &c. ſhall reap, ſhall reap, ſhall, &c.
joy, &c. for they that ſow in tears, &c.
The dying Chriſtian's laſt farewell. Spoken in the tenor.
Fare you well,
Fare you well,
My friends I am going a long journey never to return, Farewell,

:S:

And God grant we may meet in that land of harmony where the wicked ceafe from troubling and

Fare you well my friends,

1 2

where the weary are at reft Where pleafures dwell for - ev - er more, and joys that never never fade, where pleafure

and

Joy - - s that

Joys that never, never fade, where

joys that never fade, Where pleafures dwell for - ever more and joys that never fade, and joys that never fade, and
dwell forever more, and joys that never, joys that never fade, Where pleafures dwell for - ever more and joys that never
never, never' never, never, never, never, never fade, that never, never fade, that never, never
pleafures dwell for-ev - er more and joys that never, joys that never, never, fade, that never, never fade, where
joys that never, never fade, where pleafures dwell forever more and joys that never fade, that never, never
fade, and joys that never fade, Where pleafures dwell forever more and joys that never never fade, where pleafures
fad , that never, never fade, and joys that never, never fade, that
pleafures dwell forever more and joys that never fade, that never, never fade, that never, never

fade, and joys that never fade, where pleasures dwell forevermore, and joys that never fa - -
dwell forevermore, and joys that never :||: fade and joys that never fade, where pleasures dwell forevermore, and
never, never fade, tha: never, never fade, that never, never fade, and jo - - -
fade, and joys that never fade, and joys that never :||: :||: fade where pleasures dwell forevermore, and joys that
:S:
- de, and joys that never fade, that never fade,
joys that never fade, and joy that never, never fade,
- - oy that never :||: :||: fade. My friends I am summon'd to appear at the great tribunal,
never :||: fade, and joys that never, &c.

:S:

Affettuoso.

Fare you well my friend,

Fare you well my friend, Languishing. and God grant we may meet in that land of

Fare you well my friend,

Fare you well my friend,

Affettuoso. Minum beating.

.Harmony, where the wicked ceaſe from troubling and where the weary are at reſt. farewell, farewell, farewell,

New-Plymouth. Words by Tate and Brady.

Suitable to be fung on the Anniverfary of our Forefathers' landing in New England, Nov. 20th. Anno Domini 1620.

☞ Roufe ye Yankies and celibrate this Anniverfary, and do not fay on the sift day of November, 'I forgot what day it was yefterday.'

X

1 2
Dif - peopl'd by repeated ftrokes, Of thy avenging hand, of thy, &c.
Dif - peopl'd by repeated ftrokes, Of thy avenging hand, of thy a - veng - ing hand.
peopl'd by re - peated ftrokes of thy a - venging hand, Dif - peopl'd by repeated ftrokes of thy, &c.
thy avenging hand, Dif - peopl'd by re - peated ftrokes of thy avenging hand, of thy, &c,
Victory. Words by Dr. Watts.
confound the foe, &c.
To thine allmighty arm, We owe the triumphs of the day, Thy terrors Lord confound the foe and melt their ftrength a-
confound the foe, &c.

Sublimity, an Anthem. Pfalm 19.

This fubject is both Praife and Prayer, it may anfwer for Thankfgiving or Faft.

telleth a - nother, and one night doth certify, doth certify, doth certify, doth certify a - nother.
His hands work, for there is neither
And the firmament sheweth his, &c.
The heavens declare the glory of God,

:S:
Their ſound is gone into all lands, Their ſound is gone
ſpeech nor language where their voice is not heard. Their ſound is gone out, their ſound is gone out in-
Their ſound is gone out, their ſound is gone out, their ſound is gone out in-
Their ſound is gone out, their ſound is gone out, is gone out in - to all lands, in-
to all lands, The ſtatutes of the Lord are right and rejoice the heart, and rejoice the heart, and rejoice the

:S:
:S:
Let the words of my
heart, and rejoice, and rejoice, and rejoice the heart.
Let the
Let the words of my mouth and the meditation of my
mouth and the meditation of my heart be all - ways accept - ed in thy ſight O Lord my ſtrength and my Re-
Let the words of my mouth and the meditation of my heart be allways accepted, be allways accepted in
words of my mouth and the meditation of my heart, and the meditation of my heart be allways accepted in thy ſight
heart be allways accept - ed in thy ſight,
O Lord my ſtrength, O Lord my ſtrength,

deemer, O Lord my ſtrength and my Redeemer, O Lord my
thy ſight O Lord my ſtrength and my Redeemer, be allways accept - ed in thy ſight O Lord my ſtrength and
O Lord my ſtrength and my Redeemer be allways accepted, be allways accepted, be allways accepted in thy
O Lord my ſtrength and my Redeemer, Let the words of my mouth and the meditations of my heart be, &c.
:S: :S:
ſtrength, O Lord my ſtrength and my Redeemer.
my Redeemer O Lord my ſtrength and my Redeemer. Hallelujah, hallelujah, hallelujah, Hal - le -
ſight O Lord my ſtrength and my Redeemer.
Amen,

:S:
Amen, Hallelujah, :||: :||: Amen.
lujah, Amen, :||: Hallelujah, :||: :||: Amen, Amen Amen.
A - - - - - men.
Amen, Hal - le - lu - jah, :||:
An Anthem. Pſalm 108. For Thankſgiving Day Morning.
O
O God my heart is fixed I will ſing and give praiſe,
O God my heart is fixed I will ſing and give praiſe,
O

God my heart is fixed, I will ſing and give praiſe, O God my heart is fixed I will ſing and give praiſe
Even with my glory,
Even with my glory, even with my glory, even with my
Even with my glory,

:S:

Awake lute and harp, I myſelf will A-
Awake, A - wake lute and
glory, even with my glory, even with my glory, Awake, Awake, lute and har-
Awake, A - wake, Awake lute and
wa - - ke, I myſelf will awake, I myſelf will A - wake will A - wa - - ke, I my-
harp, I myſelf will awake, I myſelf will Awake, will awake, I myſelf will awake,
- p, I my - ſelf will awake, I myſelf will awake, I my - ſelf will awake, will awake a-
harp, I myſelf will awake, I myſelf will awake, I myſelf will awake, I myſelf

:S:
ſelf will awake, I myſelf will awake, I myſelf will awake right early.
will awake, I myſelf will awake right early.
wake right ear - ly, right early.
will awake, I myſelf will awake, &c. I will praiſe thee O Lord a-
:S:
And I will ſing praiſ - es unto thee a - mong the nations. Be thou exalted
mong the nations.

and thy glory thy, &c.
high, be thou exalted high O God above the heav'ns, and thy glo - ry above all the earth, thy glo - ry, thy
:S:
glo - ry a - bove all the earth.
Give us help from trouble,
Give us help from

Give us help from trouble,
Give us help from trouble,
Give us help from trouble, for va- -
trouble,
for va - -
for vain, for vain, for vain, &c.
for vain, for vain is the help of man. Through God
- - - - - in, &c.
- in, for vain, for vain, for vain, &c.

we ſhall do valiantly, we ſhall do valiantly, we ſhall do valiantly, for it is
for it is he that ſhall
Through God
for it, &c.
he that ſhall tread down our enemies, for it is he that ſhall tread down our enemies, for it is he that ſhall
trerd down our enemies, through God we ſhall do valiantly, we ſhall do valiantly, for, &c.
we ſhall do valiantly for it is he that ſhall tread down our enemies, for, &c.

tread down our enemies, our enemies, our enemies, for it is he that ſhall tread down our enemies.

:S:

through God we ſhall do valiantly, for it is he that ſhall tread down our enemies. Hallelujah, halle-

lujah, :‖: Amen, Hallelujah, :‖: :‖: Amen, :‖: :‖: Hallelujah, Amen.
St. Andrew's. Words by Dr. Watts.
Behold the glories of the Lamb, Amidst his father's throne, Prepare new honours, prepare new honours for his name, And

:S:
Prepare new honours for his name, And songs, &c.
songs before unknown.
Prepare new honours for his name, And songs before unknown.
Prepare new honours for his name, And songs be - fore unknown.
Prepare new honours for his name, And songs before unknown, And songs, &c.
Cobbam.
Words by Dr. Watts.
:S:
Teach me the measure of my days, Thou maker of my frame; I would survey lifes narrow space, And learn how frail I am.
A
Z

ſpan is all that we can boaſt, An inch or two of time; Man is but vanity and duſt, In all his flow'r and prime.

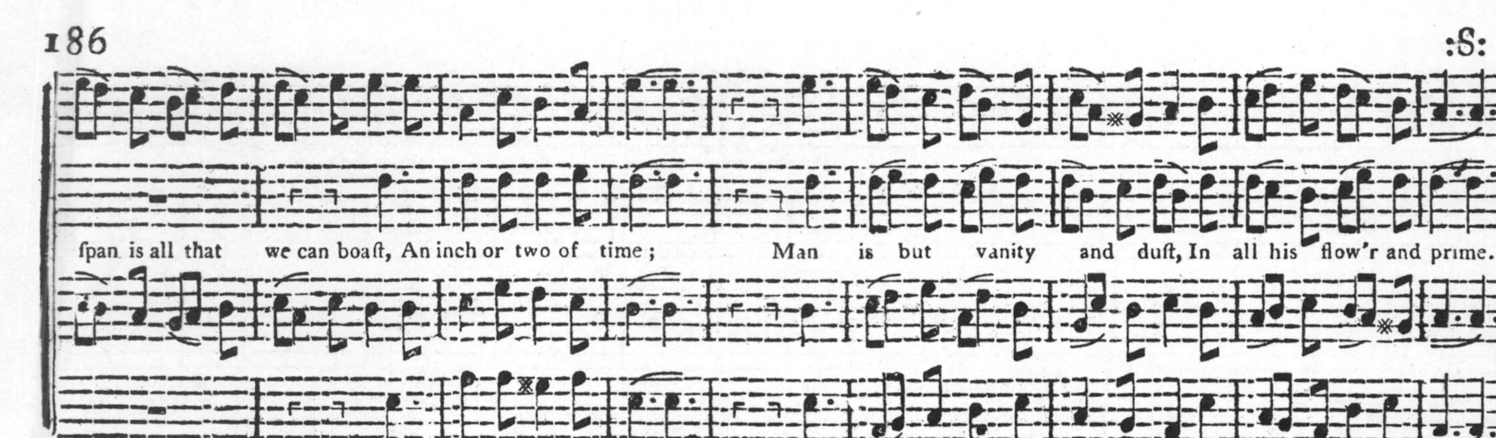

An Anthem. Joel, 1ſt and 2d Chap. Suitable for Faſt.

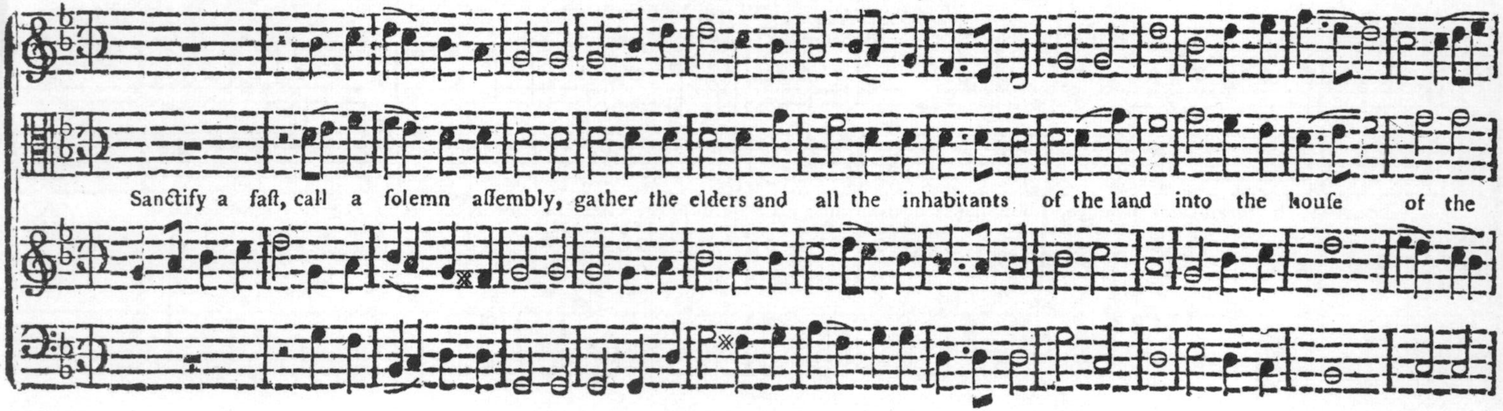

Sanctify a faſt, call a ſolemn aſſembly, gather the elders and all the inhabitants of the land into the houſe of the

Lord our God, and cry, and cry, and cry un - to the Lord,
The feed is rotten under the clods, the barns are broken
:S:
O Lord to thee will I cry, for the
How do the beasts groan because they have no pasture,
down for the corn is withered,

fire hath de - voured the paſtures of the wilderneſs, and the flame hath burnt all the trees of the field,
The beaſts of the field cry alſo unto thee,
For the rivers of water are dried up,
Blow ye the trumpet, blow ye the

Blow ye the trumpet, blow the trumpet, blow ye the trumpet, blow the trumpet,
Blow ye the trumpet, blow the trumpet, let the trumpet found, blow ye the trumpet, let the
Blow ye the trumpet, blow ye the trumpet, blow ye the trumpet, blow ye the trumpet, blow ye the trumpet,
trumpet, blow ye the trumpet, blow the trumpet, blow the trum- - pet, blow the trumpet let the
blow the trumpet, blow the trumpet, let the trumpet found.
trumpet found, found, let the, &c. Sanctify a faft, call a folemn affembly,
blow the trumpet, blow the trumpet, blow the trumpet, the trumpet in Zion.
trumpet found, found, let the trumpet found.

let the prieſts, the miniſters of the Lord weep, weep, weep, weep, between the porch and the

altar, and let them ſay O Lord, O Lord, O Lord ſpare thy people, for wherefore ſhould the heathn ſay

Sharp key.
rejoice, rejoice, rejoice, &c.
where is now their God, Fear not O land, be glad and rejoice, rejoice for the
re jo - - ice for the
rejoice, rejoice, rejoice, &c.
rejoice, re-
Lord will do great things. Be glad then ye children of Zion, and rejoice, re-
re- joi - - -
rejoice, re-

joice, :||:
joice, :||: :||: in the Lord your God.
- - ce in, &c.
joice, :||: :||: &c. For he hath given you the former rain mod'rately, and
And he will caufe to come down for you the former and the latter rain in
he will caufe to come down, &c.

And the fats fhall overflow with wine and oil,

the firft month, Be glad then ye

And the floor fhall be full of wheat,

And re - joice, rejoice,

children of Zion, and re - joice in the Lord your God, for he hath given you the former rain

mod'rately and he will cause to come down for you the former rain and the latter rain in the first month, and
praise, praise, &c.
ye shall eat in plen - ty, and be satisfy'd, and praise the name of the Lord your God. Be glad then ye

And rejoice, re - joice, rejoice, &c.
children of Zion, rejoice, :‖: :‖: in the Lord your God, for he hath given you the
And re - joi - - - - ce, &c.
And rejoice, :‖: :‖: &c.
former rain mod'rately, and he will cauſe to come down for you the rain, the former rain, and the latter rain in

And it ſhall come to paſs that whoſo - ever ſhall call on the name of the Lord,
the firſt month.
our God ſhall be de - liver - ed,
and rejoice, and rejoice,
Be glad then ye children, of Zion,
re - joice,
And re - joi - -
And rejoice, :‖:

and rejoice, and rejoice, &c.
rejoice, rejoice, in the Lord your God, for he hath given you the former rain mod'rately and
ce, &c.
re - joice, re - joice, &c.
he will cause to come down for you the rain, the former and the latter rain in the first month.
3

198
Lewis-Town.
Words by Tate and Brady.
How vaſt muſt their advantage be, How great their pleaſure prove ; Who live like brethren, And conſent in offices of
love, 'Tis pleaſant as the morning dew, That fell on Zion's hill ; When God his mildeſt glory ſhews, And

makes his grace dis - til. Tis like the oil di - vine - ly sweet, On Aaron's rev'rend

head, The trick'ling drops perfum'd his feet, And o'er his garments spread.

INDEX.

ANTHEMS.

* This tune fhould be named Sudbury, not Weft Sudbury.

THE JOHN HARVARD LIBRARY

The intent of
Waldron Phoenix Belknap, Jr.,
as expressed in an early will, was for
Harvard College to use the income from a
permanent trust fund he set up, for "editing and
publishing rare, inaccessible, or hitherto unpublished source material of interest in connection with the history, literature, art (including minor and useful art), commerce, customs, and manners or way of life of the Colonial and Federal Periods of the United States . . . In all cases the emphasis shall be on the presentation of the basic material." A later testament broadened this statement, but Mr. Belknap's interests remained constant until his death.

In linking the name of the first benefactor of Harvard College with the purpose of this later, generous-minded believer in American culture the John Harvard Library seeks to emphasize the importance of Mr. Belknap's purpose. The John Harvard Library of the Belknap Press of Harvard University Press exists to make books and documents about the American past more readily available to scholars and the general reader.